W9-DCV-041

THE GOLDEN
GEOGRAPHY

TIME AROUND THE WORLD
The time of day or night at any place in the world, at any given time, is measured from the Prime Meridian. This imaginary line runs north and south to the poles, passing through the location of the Greenwich Observatory in England. When it is noon at Greenwich, the time around the world is as these clocks show it to be.
night
morning
1
2
3
4
5
6
7
8
9
10
11
Prime Meridian
Prime Meridian
D395395

afternoon
evening
night
midnight
14
15
16
17
18
20
21
22
23
24
International Date Line
International Date Line

The Golden GEOGRAPHY

A Child's Introduction to the World

BY ELSA JANE WERNER
PICTURES BY CORNELIUS DE WITT

SIMON AND SCHUSTER • NEW YORK

A NOTE TO PARENTS

The world of the child of today is much larger than that of the child of a generation ago. Through newspaper, radio, movies, and television he is daily exposed to ideas about distant lands and even other planets in a confusing mixture of fantasy and fact.

Here is a book to clarify his ideas on some of these subjects, give him fundamental information, and stimulate him to seek further knowledge.

Here are lively but factual pictures of the arctic, the tropics, moist jungles and dry deserts, and rugged mountain peaks. The simple text helps the child understand why the climate is different in these various kinds of settings, why the seasons are different from those he knows, and how these differences shape the lives of people living there.

Large, puzzling concepts such as night and day, the seasons, and basic topographical features of the earth are briefly, concisely presented. The emphasis of the book is on helping the child move out into his great, ever-expanding world of experience with a feeling of friendly confidence devoid of prejudice and fear.

MARY M. REED, PH.D.
Formerly of Teachers College
Columbia University

Our earth moves around the sun. *As it moves, the earth spins like a top.*

 DESIGNED AND PRODUCED BY THE SANDPIPER PRESS AND ARTISTS AND WRITERS GUILD, INC. PRINTED IN U.S.A. BY WESTERN PRINTING AND LITHOGRAPHING CO. PUBLISHED BY SIMON AND SCHUSTER, INC., ROCKEFELLER CENTER, NEW YORK 20. PUBLISHED SIMULTANEOUSLY IN CANADA BY MUSSON BOOK CO., LTD., TORONTO

Our earth spins like a top.

OUR EARTH

This is our earth.

It is a huge round ball, spinning in space. It spins like a top with a stick poked through from top to bottom. The spots where the stick would come out at the top and bottom of the earth we call the poles—the north and south poles.

The earth is tilted a little, as you can see in the picture. It is always tilted the same amount and in the same direction.

Of course we never see the whole earth like this. To see the round ball of the earth spinning in space, we would have to fly thousands of miles out into the sky in some new kind of rocket.

Then we could see one whole side of the earth. And perhaps through the cloudy layer of air around the earth we could see the wide oceans, with patches of land between.

We have day when we face the sun, night when our part of the earth turns away from its light.

NIGHT AND DAY

Our earth gets its warmth and light from the sun. The sun is a huge blazing ball, many times larger than the earth. And it is millions of miles away.

The earth spins around once every twenty-four hours. So most of the earth turns to face the sun and spins away again during every twenty-four hours.

morning

noon

If the earth were the size of the small ball, the sun would be much larger than this big circle, if it were completed.

When our part of the earth faces the sun, we see sunlight and have day. When our part turns away from the light, we have night.

When our part begins to turn toward the sun and we see the first sunlight, we call it morning.

When we are facing the sun most directly, it is noon. Then the sun is closest to being straight above us. When we begin to turn away from the sun, we have afternoon and evening. And night. This happens to most parts of the earth in each twenty-four hours.

evening

night

The earth and other planets travel around the sun.

We get more heat from the sun's rays when they shine straight down upon us.

THE SEASONS

There are nine great balls traveling in great circles around our sun. Our earth is one of these balls. Each ball is called a planet. With the sun, the nine planets make up our solar system.

Our earth takes 365¼ days to travel around the sun. This makes our year.

As the earth travels around, first one pole and then the other is tilted toward the sun. When the north pole is toward the sun, the sun shines right across the north pole and the hot rays shine down quite straight on the northern part of the earth. They slant down toward the southern part.

The slanting rays cover a much larger section of the earth's surface than the same number of rays coming straight down. The more the rays are spread out, the less heat they give to the part of earth they touch.

Also, the blanket of air around the earth takes up some of the sun's heat. When the rays come at a slant, they go through more of the blanket of air. They lose more heat. They are more spread out. We get less heat. And we have colder weather.

When the north pole tips toward the sun, the sun's rays shine straighter down on the northern half of the world. It is warmer and has its summer (June, July and August). It also has longer days, because it faces the sun more of the time.

When the south pole is toward the sun, the southern half of the world is warmer, and it has its summer (December, January, February). Then the northern half is getting less direct sunshine, because it tips away from the sun. It has shorter days. It has winter.

The seasons between we call spring and autumn or fall.

spring

summer

autumn

winter

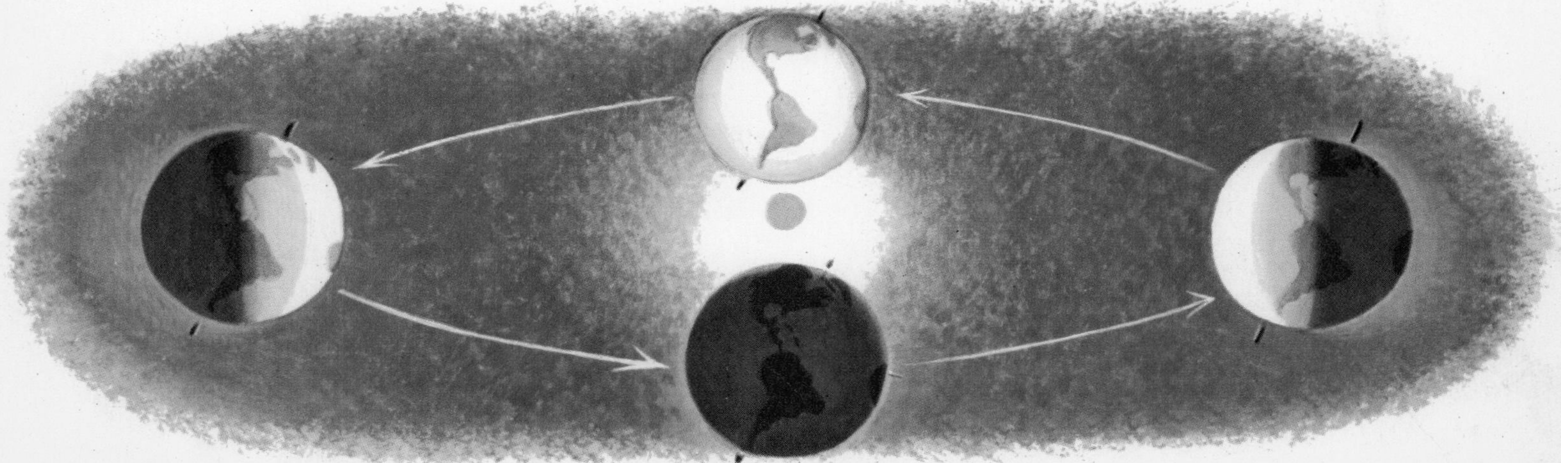

The earth's crust, with mountains and valleys, is as smooth for its size as a rubber ball.

WHAT THE EARTH IS MADE OF

Our earth is a great ball 25,000 miles around. The earth is much bigger compared to the size of a person than your schoolhouse would seem to an ant.

Probably at one time the earth was blazing hot, like the stars we see in the sky at night. Probably then it gave off light and heat and sparkled from far off, like a star. That was billions of years ago.

Through the ages the earth has cooled. But there is still fiery hot rock deep inside.

Toward the outside, the rock is cool and hard. There are layers and blocks of many different kinds of rock. Some are harder and heavier than others. And they are of many different colors.

On the very outside of the earth is a bumpy crust of rock and soil. We look at those bumps—the mountains and valleys around us. We think of the deep lakes and oceans. And we think that the earth's crust is very uneven indeed. Actually, even with its highest mountains and deepest ocean spots, the earth is as smooth for its size as a rubber ball.

Covering much of the earth's surface is a blanket of water. And all around the earth is a blanket of air, many miles thick. This air we call the atmosphere. We breathe it, and it gives us our weather.

The air is always moving. The movements of air make our winds. Tiny drops of water in the air form clouds. And as the clouds move about they bring us rain and snow and storms.

We know that the air holds some of the warmth coming from the sun. Without the air to stop some of the sun's heat, every part of the earth would be burning hot during the day when the sun's rays struck it.

Without the air to hold some of the sun's heat, the earth would be freezing cold at night, too cold for us to live.

THE STARS AND MOON

At night we like to see the pale light of the moon and the twinkling stars.

The stars are really huge suns like our sun, but they are farther away in space. Some of them have other balls like our earth traveling around them in space.

The stars are so fiery hot that they give off great light and heat—more than the hottest, brightest fire you can imagine. This firelight travels faster than we can imagine. But the stars are so far away that their light still takes years to reach us.

Look up at the stars tonight. The light you see coming from some far-off stars started on its journey more than a hundred years ago.

The moon is a ball of cold rock. It is much smaller than the earth. It circles around the earth as the earth circles around the sun.

Since the moon is cold, it does not shine with light of its own. We can see it only when the sun is shining on it, or when sunlight is reflected on to it from the earth.

When the side of the moon on which the sun is shining is facing us, we see a round shining circle—a full moon.

Sometimes the sunny side of the moon is only partly turned toward us. We see just half of the circle shining. The other half turned toward us is dark. When the moon is like this, we call it a quarter moon.

Sometimes the sunny side of the moon is turned away from us. We may see only a sliver of light along one edge. We call this a new moon.

The whole journey of the moon around the earth takes twenty-eight days. We see the change from new moon to quarter to full and back to new moon every twenty-eight days. Our word month comes from the word moon.

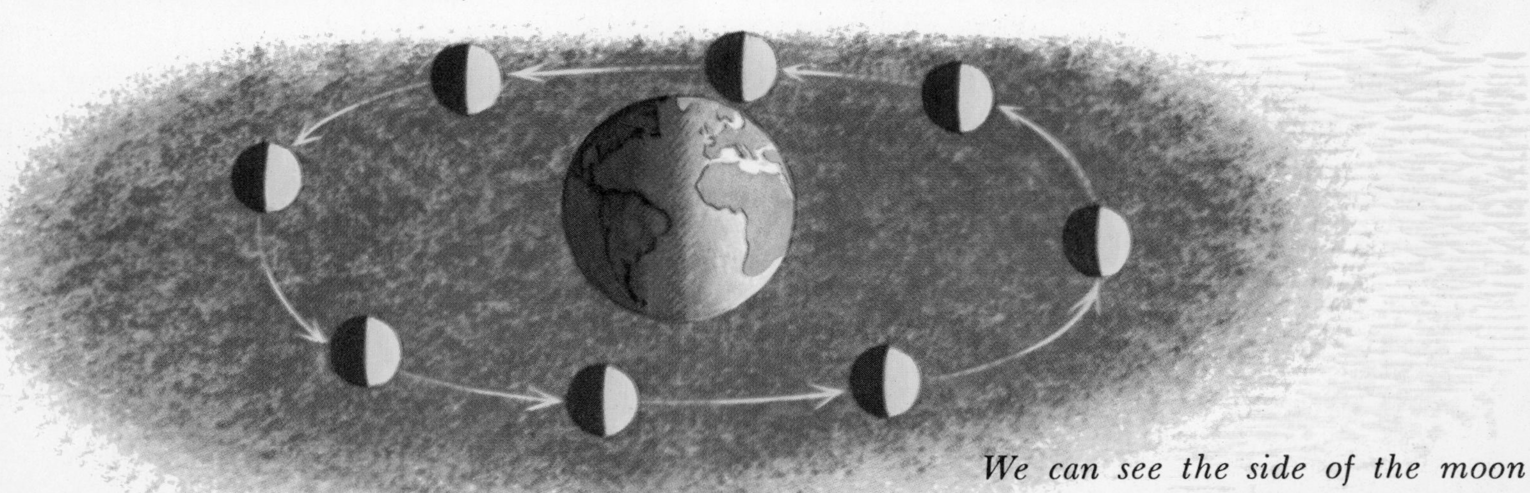

We can see the side of the moon facing us only if the sun is shining on that side.

The wind, blowing sand against these rocks for thousands of years, has worn them into strange shapes.

HOW THE EARTH'S SURFACE CHANGES

The shape of the earth's crust is always changing. Usually the change is so slow that we do not see it. Enough change for us to notice may take hundreds or thousands of years.

Water and wind are always at work. Water carries away soil and wears down rocks. Freezing water splits rocks. Wind, blowing loose sand and dirt, rubs down sharp edges bit by bit. It can even round off sharp mountain peaks. Wind also can build up hills of loose sand and dirt.

If wind and water had their way, some day all the surface of the earth would be flattened down almost to the level of the oceans.

But there are other forces at work,

Water has been wearing these rocks away through long ages.

This land was once at the bottom of a sea.

Sometimes you may find seashells in rocks like this.

building up the land. Layers of new rock are formed, through long ages, at the bottom of the oceans. Then as parts of the earth's crust shift, some layers may be pushed up above the water. They may become a high flat tableland. Or they may be crumpled like paper into a great new sharp-peaked mountain range.

It seems that slowly, slowly, some parts of the earth are always sinking. And others are just as slowly rising.

Some changes are faster. Through a crack in the earth, hot gases and blazing hot melted rock may burst out. This melted, or molten, rock is called lava. It spreads over the land. Sometimes it piles up around the hole from which it flows into a sharp-pointed hill or mountain. This is called a volcano.

Lava pours down the sides of volcanoes.

TELLING DIRECTIONS

We have spoken of the north and south poles. But how do we know which way is north and which way is south?

The easiest way to tell directions is by the sun. Do you know on which side of your house the sun rises every morning? That way or direction is East.

Do you know on which side the sun sets every evening? It is the opposite of East. It is West.

Now stand with your arms straight out at your sides. Have your right arm point East toward the sunrise. Your left arm points West. You are facing North. South, the fourth direction, is behind you.

Always remember, if the rising sun (East) is on your right hand, you are facing North. From that you can figure out the other directions.

The sun always rises in the east and sets in the west. When your right hand points east, you face north.

morning

The front of the Big Dipper points to the North Star. So does the handle of the Little Dipper.

evening

The sun gives us one way to tell directions. But some people, especially seamen, tell by the stars.

Find the Big Dipper in the sky. The two stars on the front of the dipper point to a near-by bright star. It is the North Star. The other stars seem to change their places, from where we stand. But the North Star always stays almost exactly in the same place as we see it.

Woodsmen can tell directions by the growth of plants like moss. Moss does not like the sun. So in the northern part of the earth it grows best on the north side of trees, where the sun never shines.

Moss and lichens grow best on the sunless north side of rocks and trees.

A compass can help us find directions too. A compass has a needle which always points to the north. (This is because of a force called magnetism.) Usually the needle is in a small case with a glass top, so you can see in.

The letters N, S, E, and W, which stand for the four directions, are printed below. Lay the compass flat and turn it carefully until the N for North lies under the needle's point. By looking at the other letters you can tell where the other directions are.

Hold a compass flat. Turn it until the needle points to N for north. It will show you all the directions.

To find our way from place to place, we need to know more than directions. We need to know how to read maps. Surely you have seen a road map which tells how far apart towns are, and what roads you can take from one to another.

Any map is a drawing which shows where places are in relation to each other. A map usually looks a little like a picture taken from straight up in the air.

On a larger map, cities and towns are shown by circles and dots. These do not try to show what the towns look like. They just show where they are.

Rivers are lines on a map. Mountains are often shown by rows of zigzag lines, which tell us that at that place the land is piled up into ridges and peaks. The map does not try to show what the mountains look like; it just shows where they are.

Road maps show towns and the roads between them, somewhat as tney appear from the air.

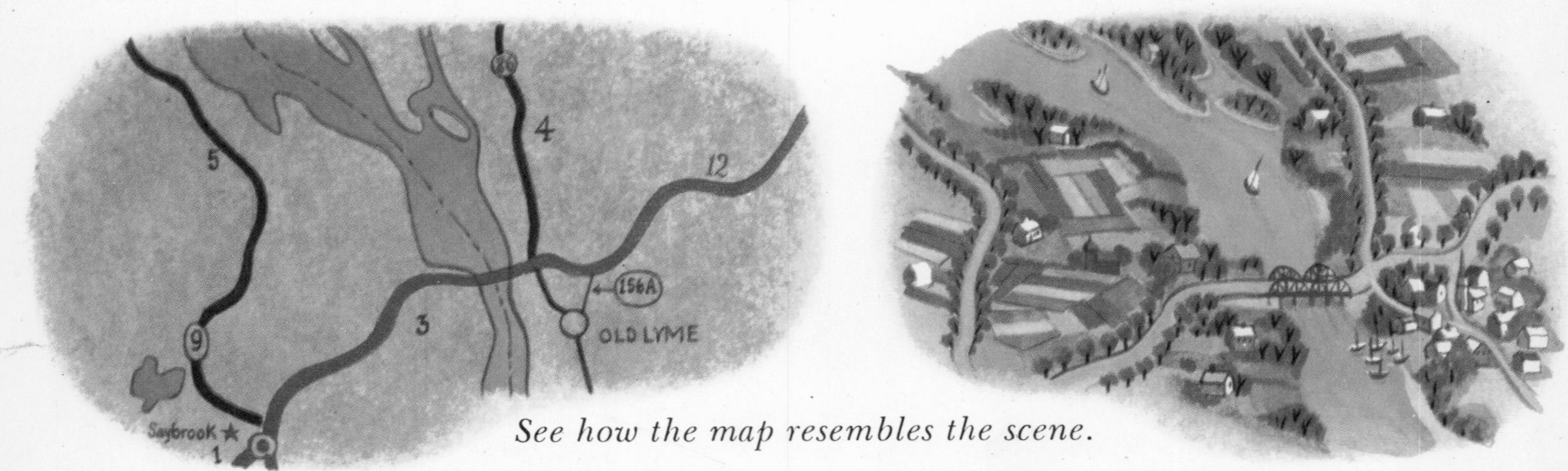

See how the map resembles the scene.

Of course a map is not really a picture. On a map of your neighborhood, the houses would be little squares. Those little squares would not show what the houses looked like. They would just show where they were. Perhaps you could draw a map of your block showing all the streets and houses.

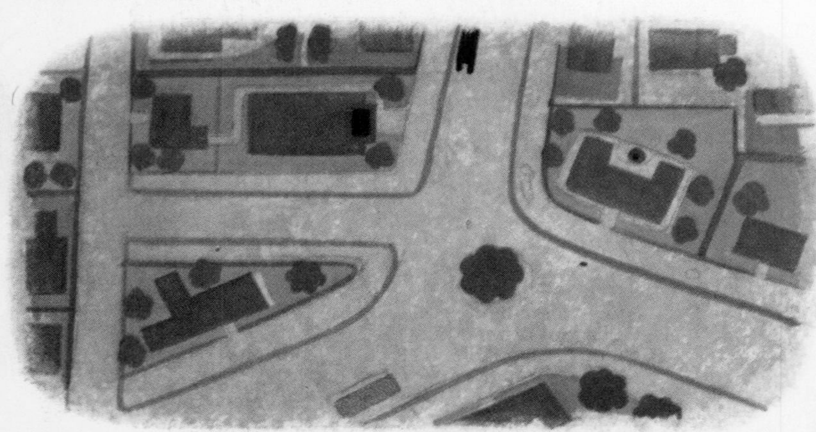

A map of the neighborhood shown at the right.

Hundreds of years ago, men were already making maps of the parts of the world they knew. In those days they thought the world was flat. They thought the ocean flowed all around the land to the edges of the world. They thought that if you sailed too far across that ocean in any direction, you would sail right off the edge of the world.

Now we know that our earth is not flat but round. We know that if we kept traveling straight ahead in the same direction for thousands of miles, we would go all the way around the earth, and come back to our starting place.

If you travel straight around the world, you will end up where you started.

It is hard to show the roundness of the world on a flat paper map. That is why the best maps of the whole earth are not drawn on flat paper but are on round balls called globes.

You can turn a globe around, just as the earth turns around every day. And you will see in turn every place on the earth, and how far each is from others.

A globe is a round map of the world.

This map tells you which parts of the land are wet and which parts of the land are dry.

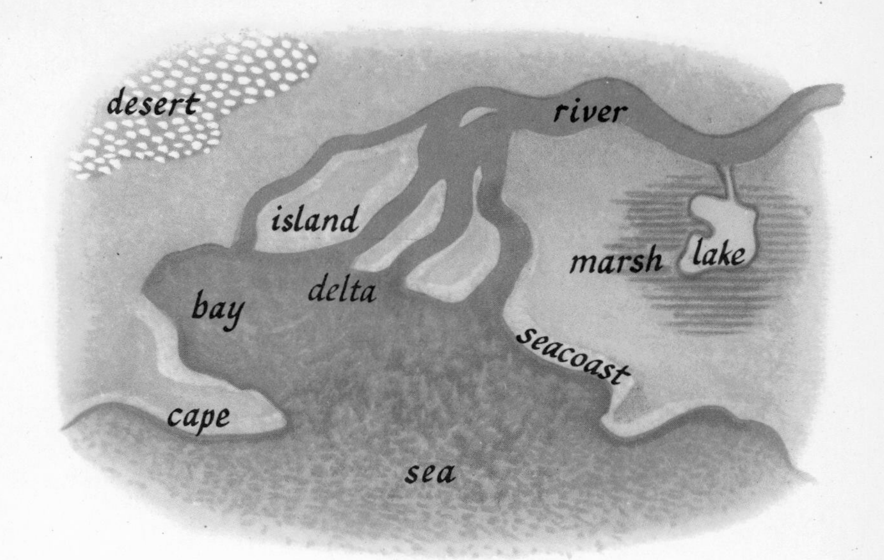

A flat map can tell you many things, though. It can tell you where and how far apart places are, and the shape of the land and rivers and great bodies of water. A map can be planned to tell you many special things — how wet or dry the land is; how high above sea level it is; what roads or railroads run across it; how large its towns and cities are.

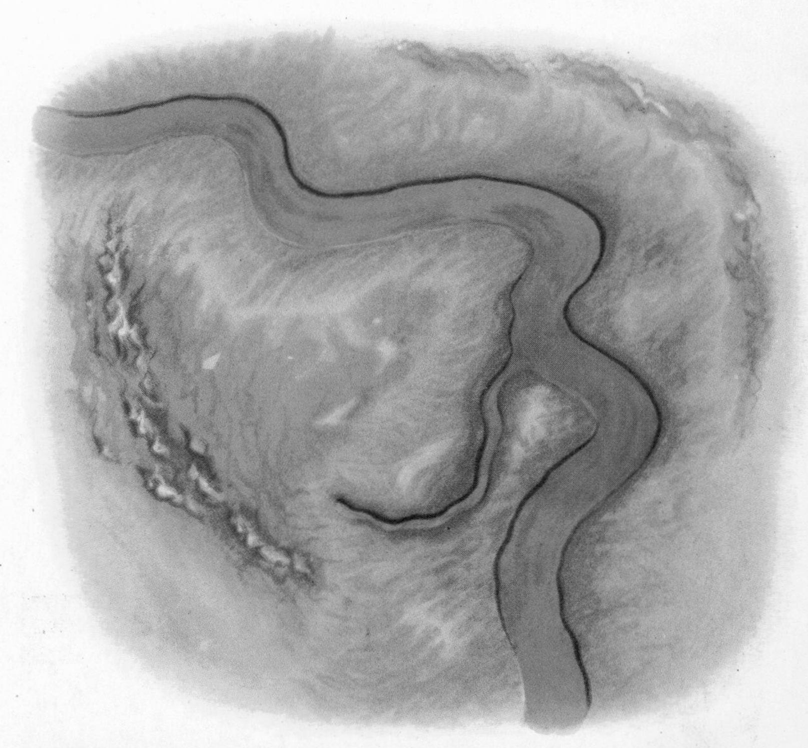

This map tells you which parts of the land are high and which parts of the land are low.

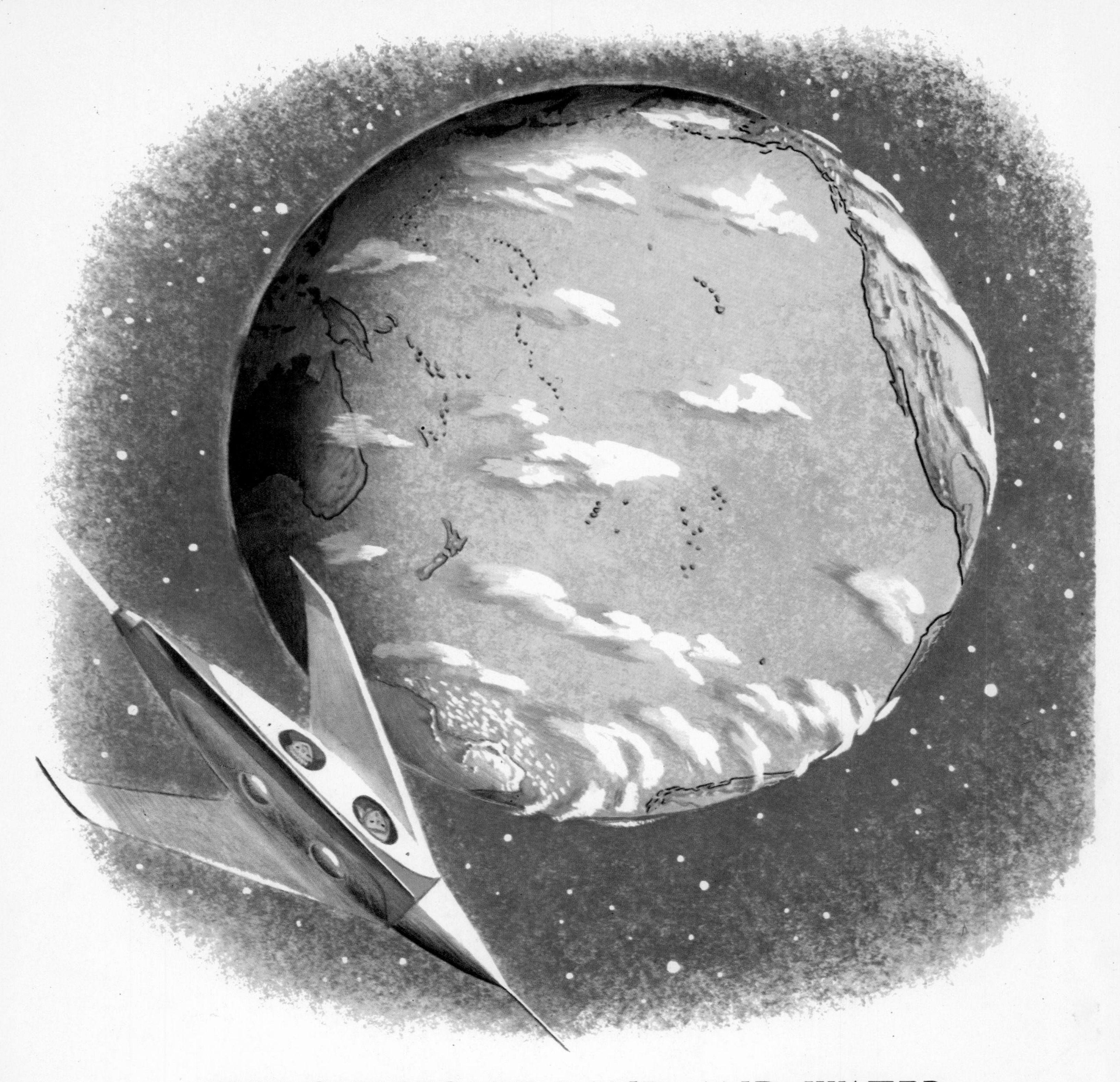

THE SHAPES OF LAND AND WATER

To look at the lands and waters of the earth as we see them on maps, we must fly up high in a rocket ship. We must go higher than the earth's blanket of air.

Trees and roads and rivers and cities fade away far below. Higher and still higher we go. Now the earth curves away at the far edges of sight. It looks more and more like a ball.

Still higher! Now far off in space we see a round ball. It is our earth. And on that ball we see pale patches and darker ones.

Those dark shapes are the great bodies of land we call continents. The continents are Asia, Europe, Africa, North and South America, Australia, and Antarctica.

The lighter patches which lie all around the continents are water. They are the oceans. The oceans are the Atlantic, Pacific, Arctic, Antarctic, and Indian Oceans.

Can you find some of these on the map above?

There is far more water than land to be seen. For every piece of land, there is almost three times as much of the earth's surface covered with water. And most of it is in the great oceans of the world.

Each of the three great oceans—the Pacific, the Atlantic, and the Indian—is much bigger than any of the continents. In fact, all the land on earth put together would not cover the surface of the Pacific Ocean.

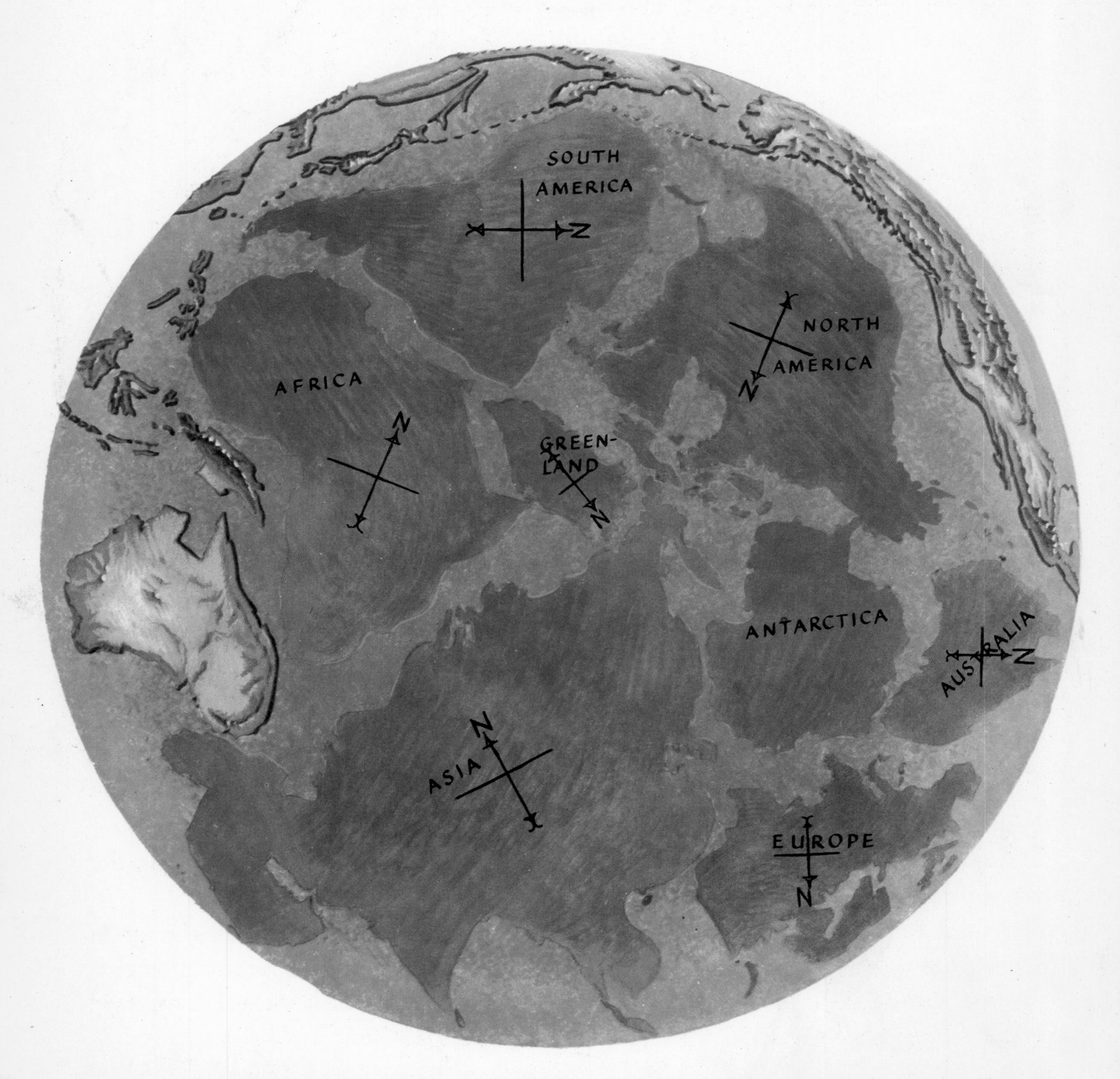

All the continents of the earth together could not cover the Pacific Ocean.

THE CONTINENTS

Here is a great block of land. It is made up of three continents: Europe, Africa and Asia. Asia is the largest of the continents.

To the west Asia tapers off into the smaller, rough-edged stretch of Europe. It is hard to say where one stops and the other begins.

Down below Europe lies the great chunk of Africa. These three continents together make up the largest connected land mass in the world.

In Turkey the young people are taking over modern European ways in dress and manners.

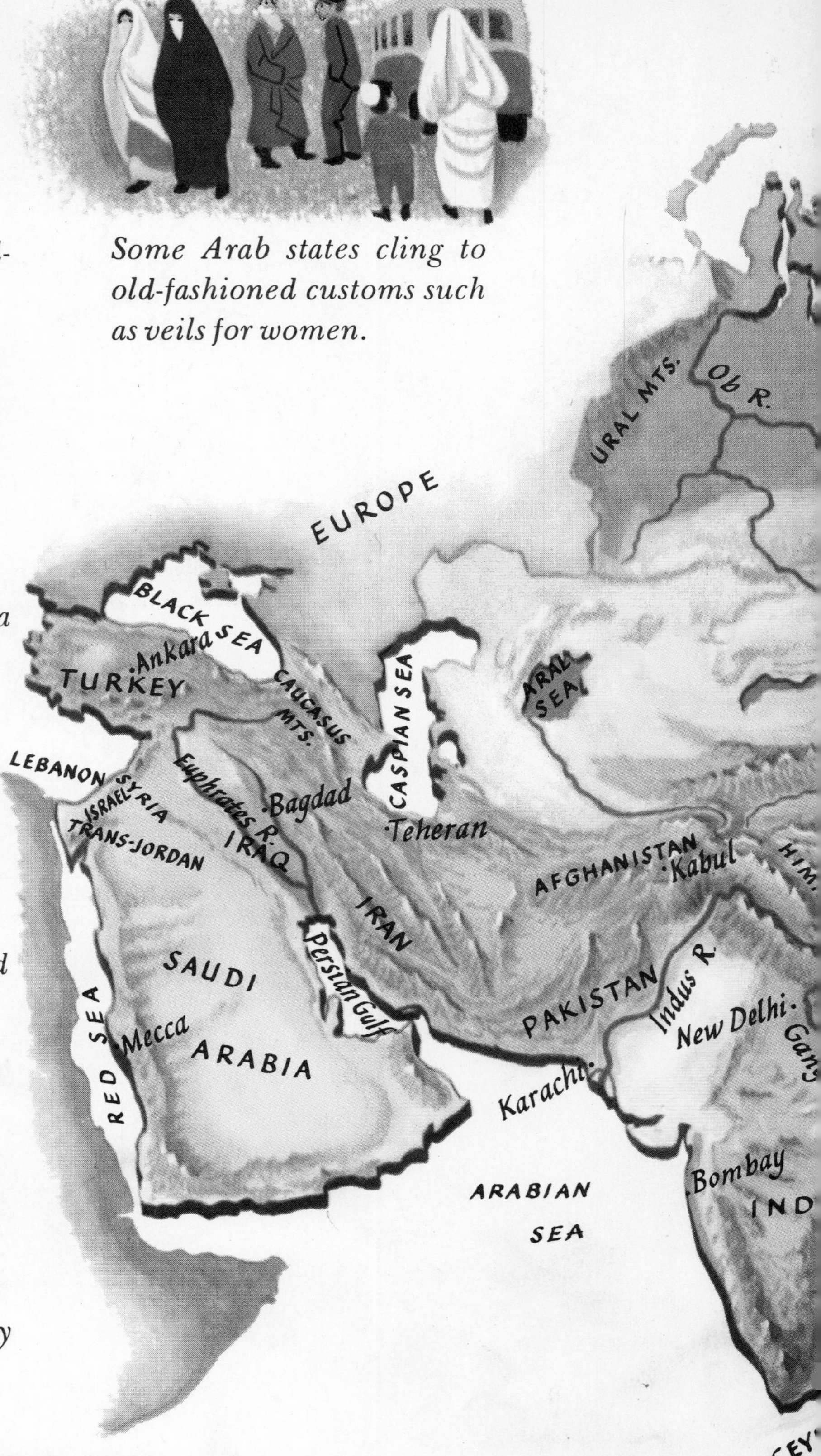

Some Arab states cling to old-fashioned customs such as veils for women.

Old and new methods in agriculture meet in Asia Minor.

The warm climate of India means that markets and most of living are in the out-of-doors.

In the high Himalayas people exchange goods by barter instead of buying and selling.

THIS IS ASIA

Asia is the largest of the continents—it goes halfway up and down the earth, a third of the way around. It has more people than any other continent. It has the world's highest mountain peak (Mt. Everest) and the world's lowest dry land (near the Dead Sea in Palestine).

Asia has some of the world's oldest and least-known nations, like the high tableland of Tibet. And it has some of the newest additions to the world family of self-ruling nations—India and Pakistan and Israel.

Asia has a huge desert, the Gobi, where even

In vast wooded stretches of Siberia a few people live in scattered villages, growing grain and seeds for oil.

Manchuria is the industrial heart of Asia. Here great factories hum.

People of China have taken over some Western ways, but there is still much Oriental color in their lives.

Many races mingle in seaport cities of Southern Asia.

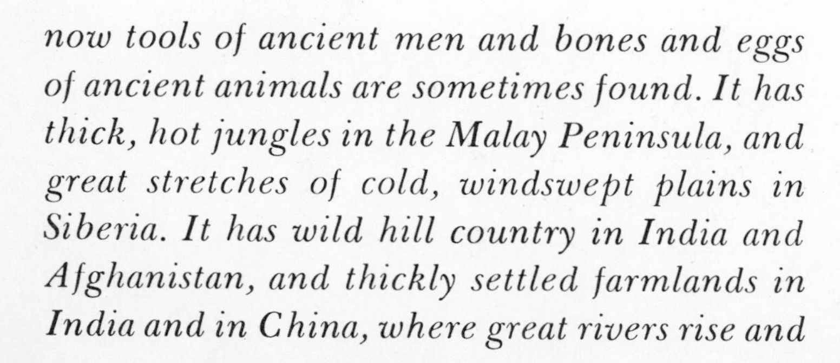

now tools of ancient men and bones and eggs of ancient animals are sometimes found. It has thick, hot jungles in the Malay Peninsula, and great stretches of cold, windswept plains in Siberia. It has wild hill country in India and Afghanistan, and thickly settled farmlands in India and in China, where great rivers rise and flood the low parts of the country every year.

Asia still has some of the world's richest rulers, with huge palaces and treasures of gold and jewels. And it has millions of the world's poorest people, who seldom have enough to eat or a chance to go to school and to grow up healthy and strong.

Jerusalem is in the part of Asia nearest to Europe. It has many mosques and other temples.

Here men are uncovering ruins of old civilizations. This digging is being done in Babylonia.

Few people visit mountainous Turkestan to see ruins like this old mosque.

Nepal, with its rich temples, is a tiny kingdom in the shadow of the Himalayas.

Tibet is one of the least-known countries in the world. This is one of its temples.

A wealthy Indian prince built the Taj Mahal in memory of his wife.

Siam has this beautiful Temple of the Dawn.

China's pagodas are many-storied towers. They often are a part of a temple.

The Chinese built their Great Wall, which is hundreds of miles long, 2,000 years ago.

On the island of Ceylon, off Asia's southern coast, is a temple to Buddha, a great religious leader.

The jungle hid this deserted temple for hundreds of years. It is called the Angkor Wat.

BAREN
ICELAND
NORWAY
SWEDEN
FINLAND
ATLANTIC OCEAN
SCOTLAND
NORTH SEA
NORTH IRELAND
GREAT BRITAIN
EIRE
WALES
ENGLAND
BALTIC SEA
DENMARK
NETHERLANDS
GERMANY
POLAND
SOVIE
English Channel
BELGIUM
Seine R.
Rhine R.
FRANCE
BAY OF BISCAY
Loire R.
CZECHO-SLOVAKIA
Danube R.
CARPATHIAN MTS.
AUSTRIA
SWITZERLAND
ALPS
HUNGARY
Rhone R.
Po R.
RUMANIA
YUGOSLAVIA
PYRENEES MTS.
PORTUGAL
SPAIN
ITALY
APPENINE MTS.
ADRIATIC SEA
Danube R.
BULGARIA
CORSICA
Balearic Islands
SARDINIA
ALBANIA
TURKEY
AEGEAN SEA
GREECE
MEDITERRANEAN SEA
SICILY

THIS IS EUROPE

Europe is a small continent. It is broken up by many high hills and mountains, curving rivers, and rough coastline. It is also broken up into many countries, about 40 of the 60 countries on earth. These have different languages and governments, different ways of doing things. And they have had many wars among themselves. But they have much in common.

The same low plains stretch across France and the low countries of Belgium, the Netherlands, and Denmark. These plains cross northern Germany and Poland to the almost endless lowlands of Russia. Most of the low plains are rich farmlands. Europe is so crowded with people that most farms are small. But the farmers work very hard on them and grow many different fruits and vegetables, grains, and even fields of flowers to sell.

There are many beautiful mountains in Europe. The Alps spread out from Switzerland into France, Germany, Austria, and Italy. Most of the land in the peninsulas of Greece, Spain, and Norway is mountainous. So all these regions have more forests and pastures for flocks and herds than large farms and cities.

In many of the mountainous countries there are swift rivers, which are used for making electric power and for lumbering. There are slow, winding streams in the flatter lands, and these are good highways for boats to travel on, carrying goods.

Europe is a very crowded continent. It has many more people for its size than any other continent. It has many large cities, humming with busy factories. These factories make all sorts of goods, from toys and tiny watches to huge machines.

Almost every one of the countries of Europe has something it makes or grows especially well, which it sends out to sell in many other lands. Some countries are famous for fruits, some for grains, some for raising fine animals. Others are famous for the products of their factories. The map on this page shows just a very few of the many, many kinds of things produced by the people of Europe.

The flat "low countries" of Northern Europe have many dairy farms.

Fields of flowers in the Netherlands grow on land lower than the sea. Great walls called dykes hold the waters back.

France has many vineyards growing grapes for wine.

Gathering cork gives these men of Spain their living.

Europe has many large cities where thousands of people work in factories, making goods and machines to be sold the world around.

The hills of Italy have many olive groves.

Sweden has many electric plants built along rushing mountain streams.

Lumbering is important in Northern Europe, from Norway across to Russia.

Except for Russia's collective farms, most of Eastern Europe has little farm machinery.

Here is one of the busy port cities along the shores of the Mediterranean Sea.

The countries of Southeastern Europe raise tobacco, along with other crops.

Threshing of grain is done by old-fashioned methods in Greece.

North Africa has busy Arab towns.

Rubber plantations have been planted in African jungles.

THIS IS AFRICA

Africa has been called the Dark Continent. This name was given to it because so much of the land has almost never been visited by white men. These unknown parts are mostly in the rough mountains and in the hot, thickly overgrown forests. More bright-colored birds and bugs and wild animals live there than people. And what people do live there are dark-skinned hunters.

Wild animals also live on open grasslands to the north and south of the jungles. And across the widest part of the continent stretch the shifting sands of the world's greatest desert, the Sahara.

Up in the north, at the mouth of the River Nile, lies Egypt, one of the oldest countries we know of. It has some busy cities. And we can visit what is left of some long-ago cities which were once as busy and as grand.

Along the Mediterranean Sea is a fringe of land where crops are grown and cities have been built.

And down at the southern tip of Africa people from Europe have found land cool enough for them to live and work in comfortably. There great mines and factories, farms and towns, have grown up, much as in Europe.

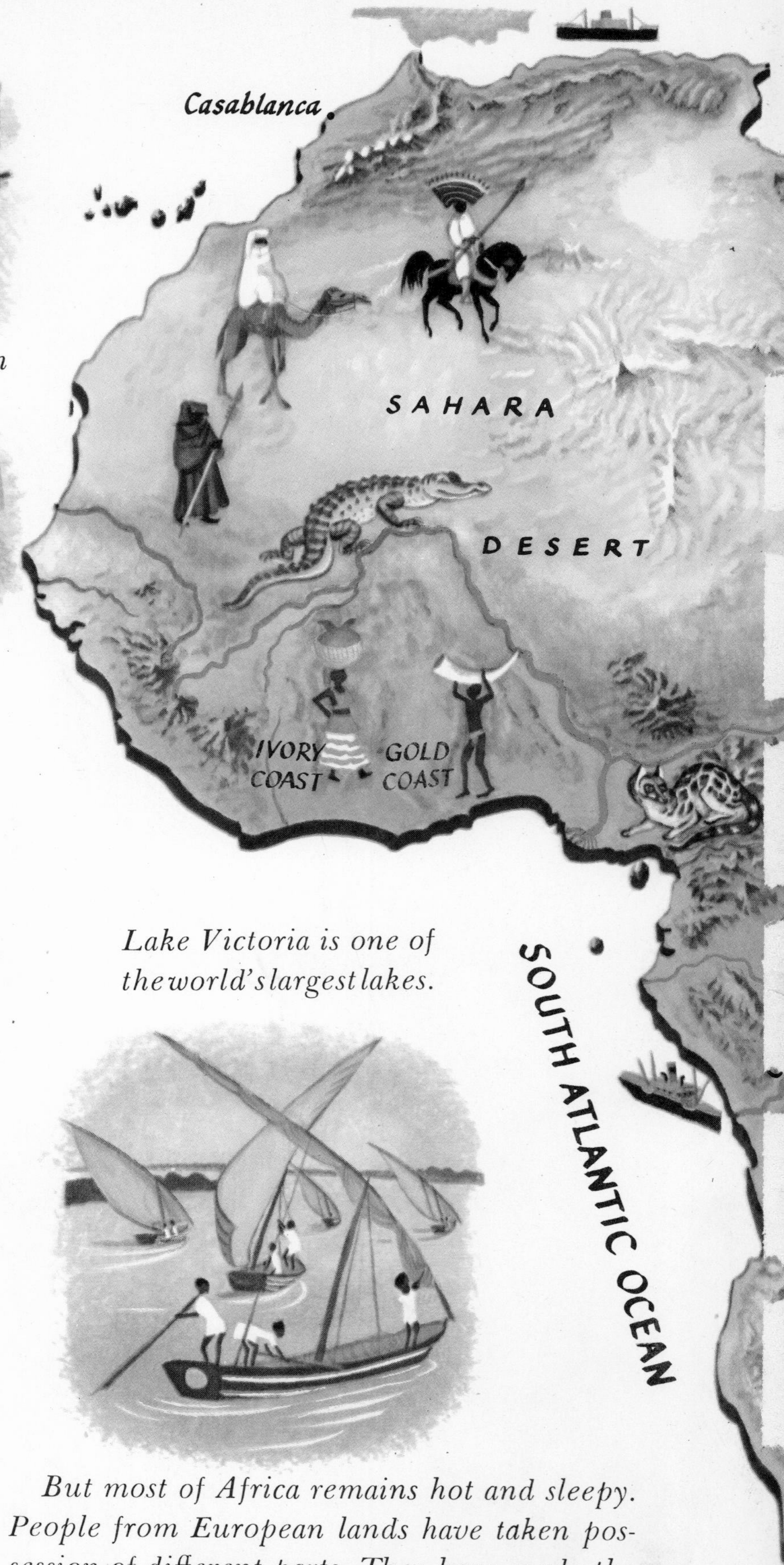

Lake Victoria is one of the world's largest lakes.

But most of Africa remains hot and sleepy. People from European lands have taken possession of different parts. They have made the people work for them. But they have not changed Africa much. It is still a land many of whose people live just as their tribes have lived for countless years, with little care for changes in the rest of the world.

Ruins of Egypt's ancient temples may still be seen.

Parts of Africa have prosperous farms. On this one peanuts are grown.

These men and animals are at home in the jungle.

Many animals use the same water holes peaceably together.

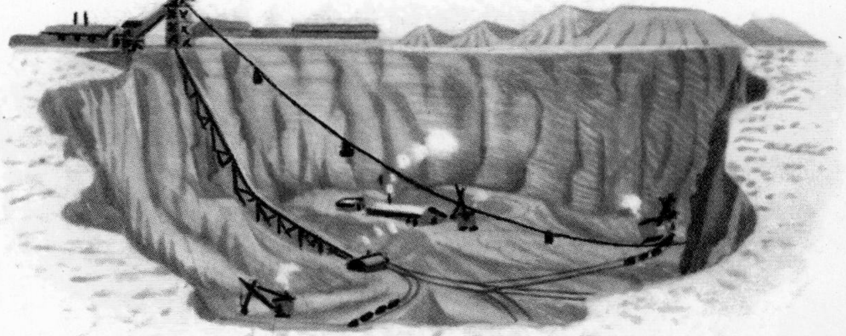

This is one of South Africa's rich diamond mines.

On we go, down around the curve of the earth until we see beneath us a wide stretch of white. This is the ice covering which hides the continent of Antarctica. And all around it flows the icy Antarctic Ocean.

Now let us fly up over the two long, three-sided continents of South and North America. This great stretch of land separates the Atlantic from the Pacific Ocean, almost from pole to pole.

Flying north from Antarctica we soon come to the cold rocky tip of South America. This continent stretches all the way up to the hot lands around the equator.

The equator is the imaginary line around the earth halfway between the two poles. There the sun shines down straightest and hottest. So the weather is always warm.

On up we go, over the length of North America. And we find ourselves above another white polar ice cap—the Arctic region of the North Pole. There is no continent beneath this ice—only a frozen ocean, the Arctic.

THIS IS ANTARCTICA

Antarctica, beneath its blanket of ice and snow, was the last land on earth to be explored. As recently as 50 years ago, people knew almost nothing of it. No one lived there. No one does to this day. For there are only icy winds and snowstorms. No plants grow there. There are few animals to be hunted for food. There are no handy building materials. And it is a very hard place to carry supplies to.

But some men began to wonder about Antarctica. They wanted to know about this frozen land. They wanted to reach the South Pole.

So groups of brave men made plans. They gathered supplies of food and clothing. They hired ships to take them as close as possible to the Pole. They took with them dogs and sleds for transportation on the rest of the journey.

Many of them died on the way. For it was a cold, hard, dangerous trip. But at last one group reached the point which they knew was the South Pole. And they got back home to tell the world.

Since then several other groups have visited Antarctica. They built small towns so they could stay awhile to study the land. They went about with dog sleds and on snowshoes. They flew over the mountains and over the Pole in airplanes. They made maps and charts. They named mountains and seas. They tested the rocks for mineral riches below. Now we know much more than before about this frozen land.

THIS IS SOUTH AMERICA

South America is an uncrowded continent. Along the west coast the world's largest chain of mountains, the Andes, runs all the way from the north to the rocky southern tip of the continent. Some fine cities have been built high in these mountains. But there is still much wild pasture land. And there are great forests of valuable woods on the mountain slopes, and plantations of coffee.

The mountains have riches under the surface, too. Copper, gold, silver, tin, and other minerals lie in the rocks, ready to be dug out.

Oil wells in this lake produce great wealth in the South American country of Venezuela.

Copper and silver are smelted into bars to be shipped to many lands.

Tobacco is grown on large plantations.

Uruguay and Argentina, two southeastern lands, have great cattle herds.

Some Indians still use old-fashioned methods of "cooking" raw rubber.

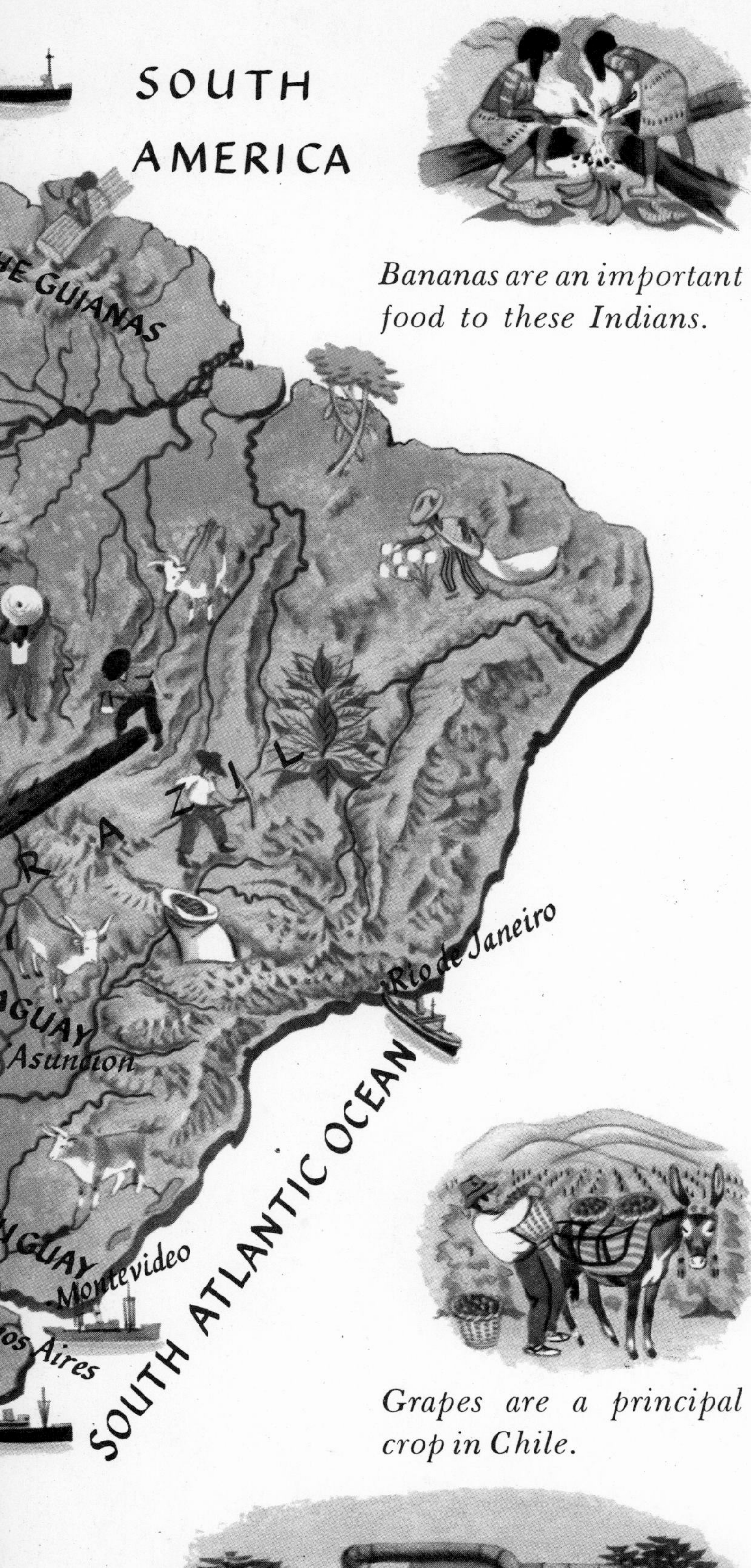

Bananas are an important food to these Indians.

Grapes are a principal crop in Chile.

Cotton is grown in Brazil, South America's largest country.

Coffee beans are one of South America's most important harvests.

The southern lands grow grains in very large fields.

There are huge, hot, damp forests in the great valleys of the Amazon and Orinoco Rivers. Hundreds of smaller rivers flow into each one of these great ones. And all through those steaming river forests scattered tribes of Indians live. Many of them have never seen a white man. But some gather rubber and cacao (cocoa) beans and bananas for white men to ship away.

South America has great plains, too. On some, called the pampas, cattle graze. Wheat and grapes and many other farm crops are grown. But there is little crowding. There is space to spare.

This space and the richness of the country have drawn people from many parts of Europe. But it was Spaniards who conquered South America's rich Indian tribes hundreds of years ago. It was Spanish settlers who built up most of the new countries. So most of the cities still have a Spanish look. And Spanish is still spoken in every country but one. Portuguese is spoken in Brazil.

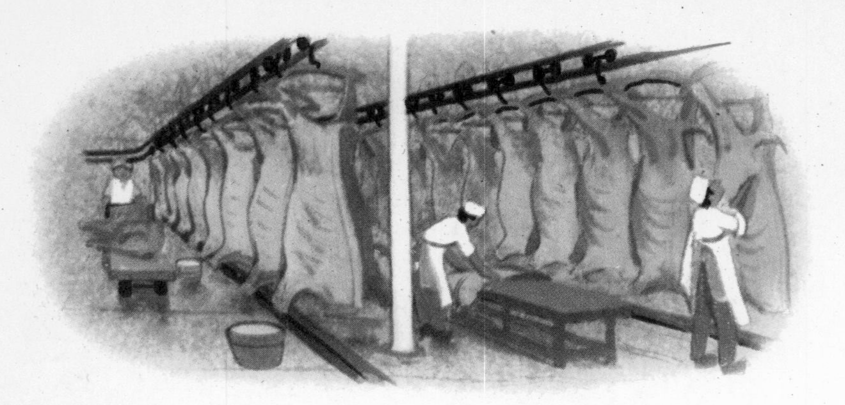

Meat packing is an important industry in South America.

Many sacks of coffee beans are shipped from these busy harbors.

Many cities in South America have beautiful open squares called plazas.

Maté leaves are gathered for tea.

Brazil nuts must be dried outside.

Cacao is an important crop.

Llamas carry heavy loads in the Andes.

SOUTH AMERICA

Nitrate found in the desert of Chile is used for fertilizer.

On the pampas live the South American cowboys, called gauchos.

Platinum and gold are mined in Colombia in the north.

Fountains and tropical plants add charm and splendor to city gardens and estates.

Rio de Janeiro is one of the most beautiful cities of South America and of the world.

Indian ceremonial dancers wear wonderful costumes.

The sisal plant gives strong fibers.

MEXICO AND CENTRAL AMERICA

The little countries of Central America are like South America in many ways. They were explored and taken over by men from Spain, long ago. But many of their people are Indians, who still live much as they did hundreds of years ago, before the Spaniards came.

These lands too have high mountains and thick forests. And like the upper half of South America, they are very hot.

Like South America, their mountain slopes grow coffee; their lowlands grow bananas and more bananas. In fact, these lands are sometimes called "the banana republics" because of their chief crop.

Mexico is attached to North America, but it is really more like South America. Its people are Indian and Spanish. Its cities are partly new, but many of them look like old Spanish towns. It, too, has hot, damp forests with banana trees and strange, bright birds and flowers. It has high, jagged mountains with scattered flocks and shepherds. It has tiny, steep mountain farms and great flat plains and deserts.

In the center of Mexico is a wide, high tableland with pleasant weather most of the time.

CENTRAL AMERICA and THE WEST INDIES

A village market in Mexico is a busy place.

Central American Indians still have old-fashioned ways of living.

There are modern sugar plantations in the West Indies.

There are many, many bananas grown in Central America.

The islands of the West Indies have some fine harbors.

Huge mahogany trees grow in Central American forests.

Central America has many colorful old Spanish towns.

In Alaska the mountains come right down to the sea.

The Southwest has forests of oil derricks.

Great grain elevators hold the wheatlands' harvest.

NORTH AMERICA

North America has mountains in the west—the Rockies. It has mountains in the east—the Appalachian chain. And between lie the Great Plains.

North of Mexico, the United States of America reaches across the continent from the Pacific Ocean to the Atlantic. For 1,500 miles from south to north, for nearly 3,000 miles from west to east, we can travel in one country.

Along the Pacific Ocean many fruits are grown. There are oranges in the south, and dates. Farther north come grapes, then apples and pears.

There is fishing along the coast. There are rich oil wells. And ships come and go from several great seaports.

Cowboys practice riding and throwing on western ranches.

Indians still hold ceremonial dances in the Southwest.

Several midwestern cities have great stockyards.

Busy harbors on the Great Lakes ship iron and copper ore and grain.

Narrow gauge railroads carry lumber through the western forests.

The West has mountains near the coast, in addition to the Rockies. The mountains have gold and silver and many rich stores of other metals. Some mountains are bare of trees and rise up from dry desert lands. Some have fine forests on their slopes, and some of these trees are cut for lumber.

Next come the great cattle ranches. Then the big flat farms, which stretch as far as the eye can see. East of these flat plains the land begins to roll. The farms are smaller, but still fine ones. Many different crops are grown here—grains, vegetables, food for milk cows, fruits, all sorts of things. Dotted among the farms are many small towns for shopping.

More cities appear in the middle of the continent, too. Most of them are built on busy rivers or on one of the Great Lakes. These cities are kept busy shipping goods in and out and buying and selling. They have factories, too, where furniture, tools, clothes, cars, and many other things are made.

Gold ore is still mined and washed in Alaska.

Lumber is sometimes towed to mills by water.

Modern dairy farms dot the Midwest.

Orange groves stretch into the California foothills.

Moving farther east we come to mountains again. These are lower and rounder than those in the West. There is coal in some. There are more forests, especially in the South. And there are swift rivers to provide electric power for factories. There are steel mills and cloth mills, factories and more factories, from the mountains to the Atlantic. Cities and more cities, people and more people. And on the very edge of the Atlantic is one of the biggest cities in all the world—New York.

Canada, too, has great mountains and swift rivers and forests for lumbering in the far West. It too has great wheat plains east of its beautiful Rockies.

Cowboys round up cattle on the western range.

Great dams are used to help turn water power into electricity.

Fishing is important along the Atlantic coast.

Life is still quiet in villages along the St. Lawrence River.

New York City has the world's tallest buildings.

Coal is mined in the eastern United States.

The Great Lakes region has open pit iron mines.

Iron is made into steel in huge mills.

Canada has rolling land with lakes and smaller farms in the middle part. And more mountains and bigger cities toward the East.

Canada runs all across North America and stretches from the United States far up into the Arctic. But most of its people live in a narrow strip just beyond the United States. North of that strip all is wilderness. There is hunting, fishing, and some mining. But few people live in this rough wooded land or in the cold Arctic wastes beyond.

Alaska stretches out into the Pacific from Canada's western edge. But it belongs to the United States. It has great snowy mountains, beautiful lakes, rushing rivers, huge forests, and some small, lively, growing cities.

The last of the continents is Australia. It lies down under the curve of the earth, where the mass of Asia breaks up into bits of land surrounded by water.

The giant gum trees of Australia seen here are important for timber, oils and dyes.

Australia has animals and plants found nowhere else in the world. Some of them are shown above.

Gold was discovered in Australia about the same time as in the United States. Many new settlers hurried to the country to hunt for gold.

AUSTRALIA

Australia is a big, open, uncrowded land. It has some fine modern cities, most of them seaports like Sydney. But beyond the Blue Mountains back of the east coast lie the wide open spaces of the continent.

There are fine fields and orchards on the great plains, and bleak mining towns.

Beyond the plains is the wild "bush" country, with scattered sheep stations, as the ranches of Australia are called. In the bush live people called "bushmen" who are different from those

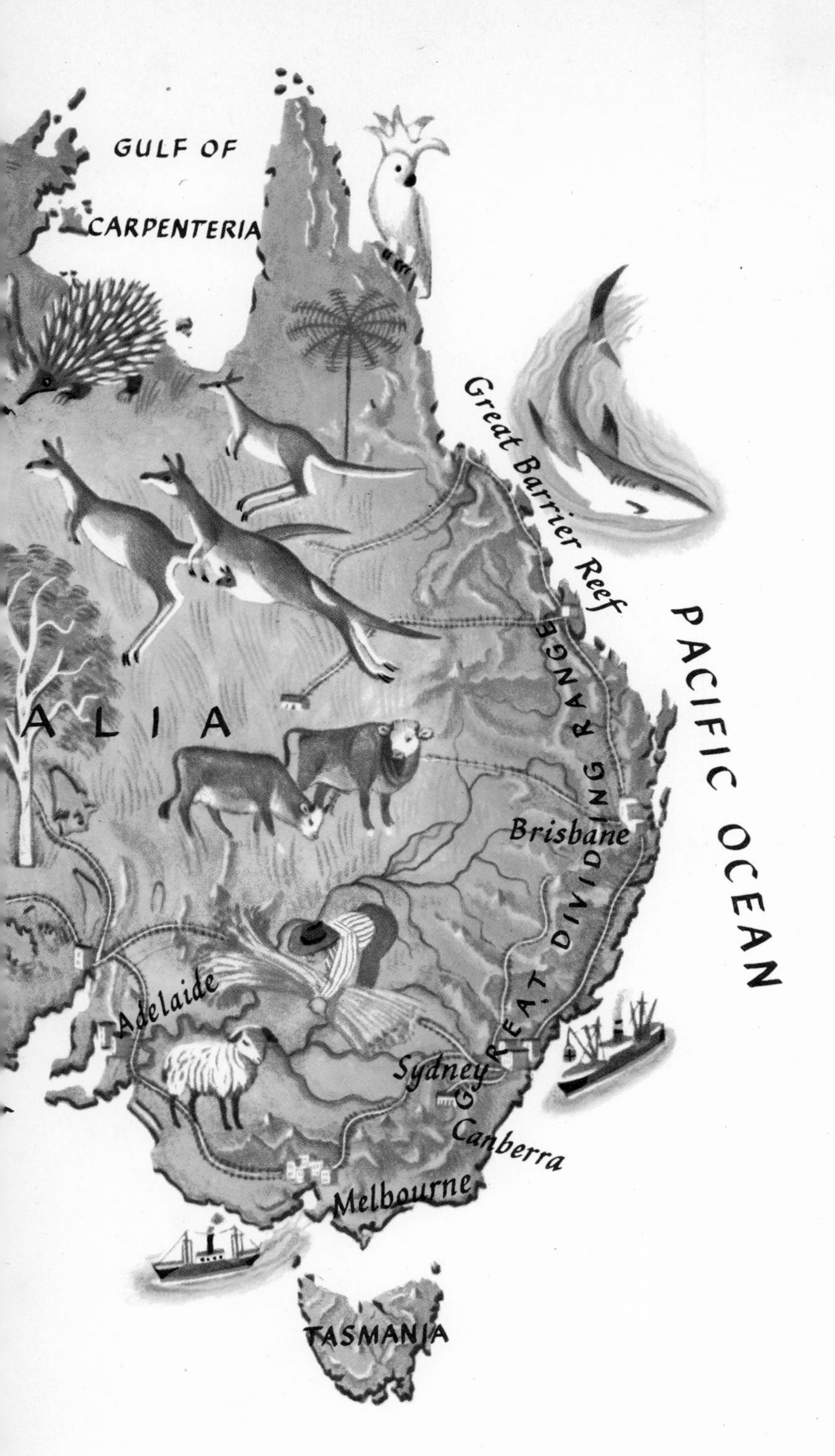

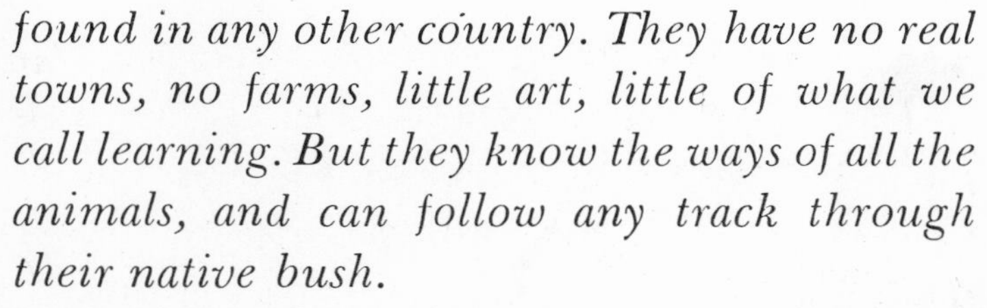
found in any other country. They have no real towns, no farms, little art, little of what we call learning. But they know the ways of all the animals, and can follow any track through their native bush.

To the north, toward the equator, are some great, thick forests. But the whole center of the continent is a great desert which is one of the least-known parts of the earth. It is very hot, dry, and hard to travel on. There are many parts no man has ever visited to this day.

Australian bushmen like to gather for a dance time called a "corroboree."

Much grain is grown on the Australian plains.

A sheep station on Australia's plains is like a North American cattle ranch.

Rabbits are a great pest in Australia. Great fences are built to keep them off the sheep range and out of farms.

The Mediterranean Sea was long the center of a busy world of trade.

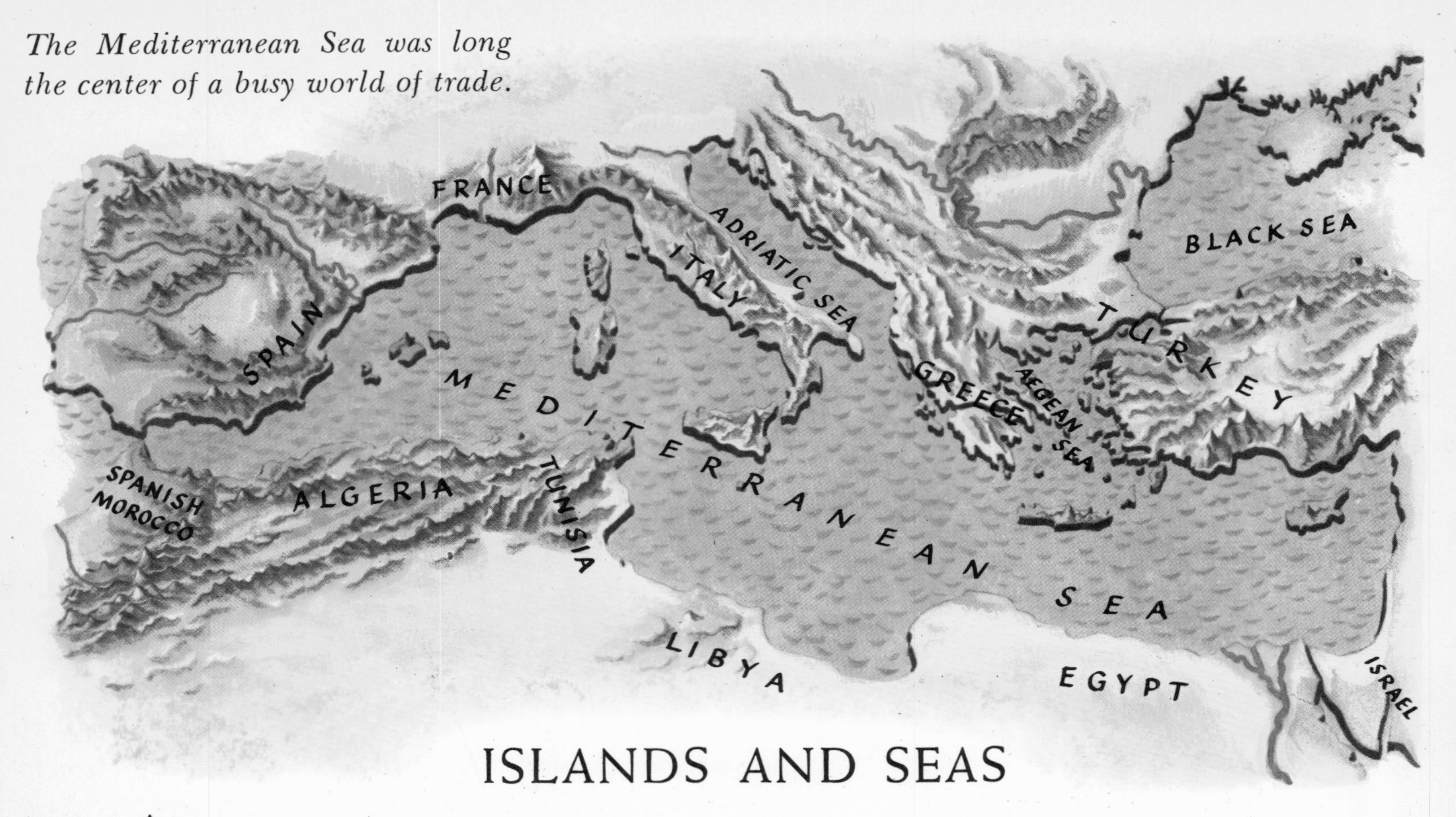

ISLANDS AND SEAS

A piece of land surrounded by water but too small to be a continent is called an island.

A large body of water surrounded by land is called a sea. A smaller one is a lake.

The oceans, as you can see on the map, are not surrounded by anything. It is often hard to say where one ends and the next begins. They flow into each other in one great stretch of water at many places. But a sea is outlined by land.

The Mediterranean is the greatest sea. It stretches between Europe and Africa, touching Asia on the east. Its name means "middle of the world." For thousands of years it was really the busy center of the world most people knew about in those days.

There are many seas. Can you find the Red Sea between Africa and Asia? (See the map on page 23.) The Caribbean between North and South America? (Map on page 40.) What other seas can you find?

Many and varied are the ships which have sailed the Mediterranean.

Fog almost always hangs low over the rocky Aleutian Islands far to the north. These islands border the Bering Sea. They stretch from Alaska, in North America, almost across to the shores of Asia.

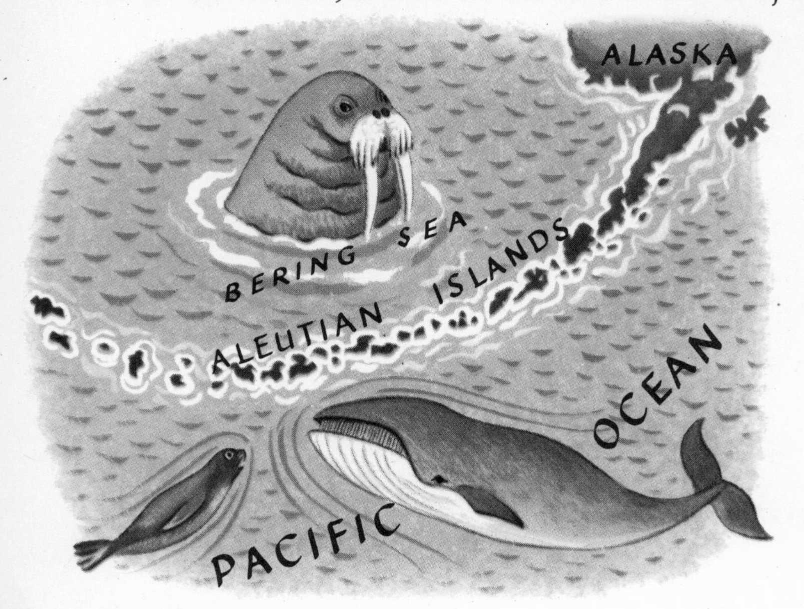

Greenland's Eskimos usually live in huts of stone, in small villages. During the short summers they raise a few vegetables. During the long winters, when no supply ships come, they hunt for seal, white whales, foxes, eider ducks, and fish.

As to lakes, they are found in every land. Some of the largest and best-known are the Great Lakes of North America. Africa has huge lakes, too. Can you find them? But everywhere there are smaller ones. Surely you have seen a lake.

Some of the islands of the world are almost as large as seas. The largest are arctic Greenland and Madagascar lying close to the eastern coast of Africa.

Many islands like the British Isles, Japan and the Philippines, are in groups.

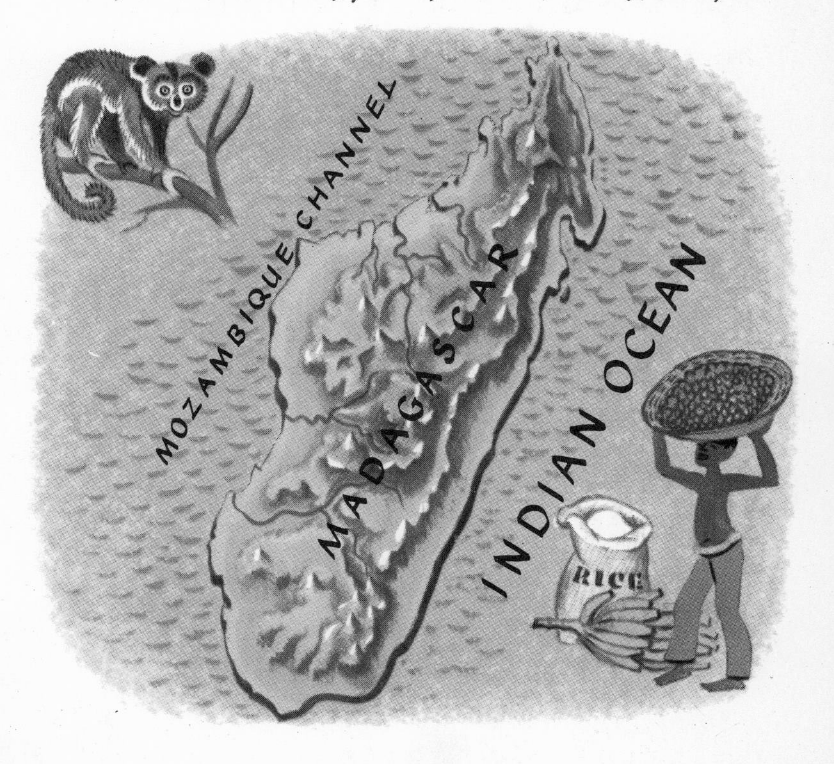

Madagascar has the simple life of lands near the equator. Houses are small, built of clay or bamboo, and roofed with branches. People wear few clothes, but they weave cloth from many kinds of threads made from plants they grow—cotton, silk, hemp, banana, and palm. Most of their foods are vegetables, since meat does not keep well in the heat.

A harbor on one of the lovely tropical islands of the West Indies. These islands border the Caribbean Sea on the east.

THE BRITISH ISLES

The British Isles are separated from Europe by the narrow English Channel. They have a mild climate, and much of the land is in farms. But still more than half the food needed for the many people crowded into busy factory cities must be brought from outside the islands.

Great Britain has long been a sea power. Many ships are built there, and they travel all over the oceans of the world, trading. Many of her men go to sea, or work in mines and factories which supply the goods those ships carry abroad.

Boating on the Thames River is a favorite pastime in southern England.

Southern England has lovely, rolling countryside.

There are busy factory towns in England's midlands.

Scotland has rugged highlands.

A shepherd watches his flock above a Scottish loch, or lake.

This is a quiet old English village.

London is one of the world's great cities.

Ireland has white-washed stone farmhouses.

Coal mining towns darken hillsides in Wales.

Sheep farms dot South New Zealand.

NEW ZEALAND

In the southern part of the Pacific Ocean, near Australia, lie the large, lovely islands of New Zealand; North and South Islands are the principal ones; small Stewart Island lies off the southern coast.

Mountain rivers grace North New Zealand.

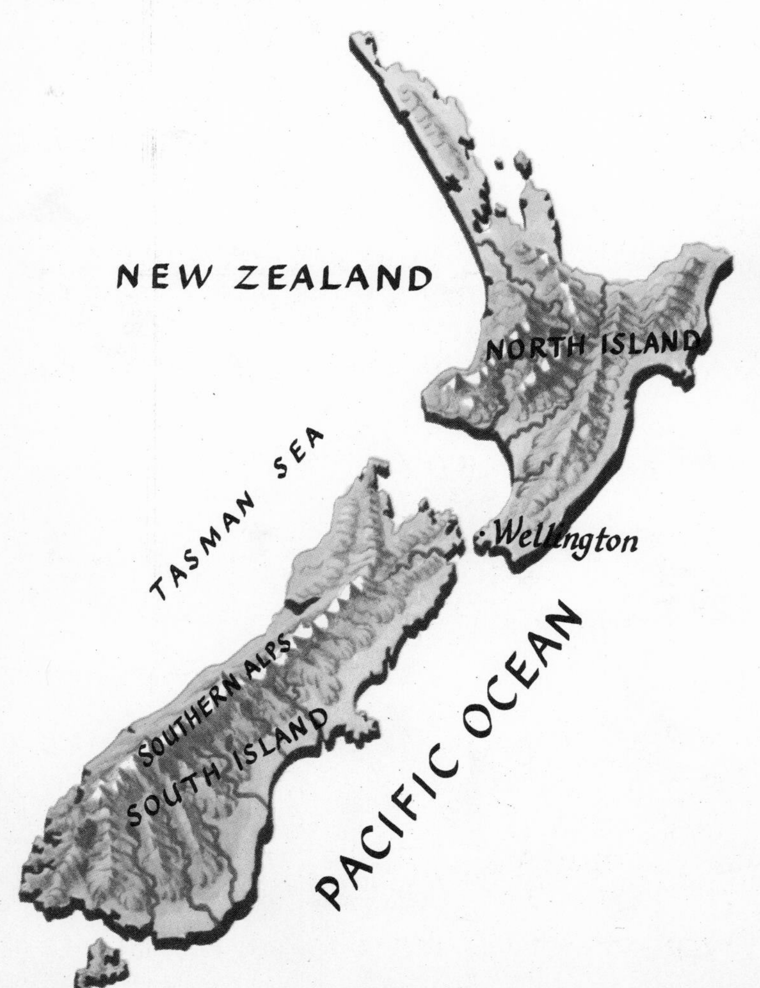

There are still Maori villages in New Zealand.

New Zealand's islands have beautiful rugged, wooded mountains, great glaciers (which are rivers of ice), snow-capped peaks, and rolling valleys dotted with herds of cattle and sheep.

New Zealand is a pleasant, unhurried place to live. It has a mild climate and good rainfall. The first white settlers found tall, light-skinned, intelligent natives called Maoris living there. There are still many of them there.

THE PHILIPPINES

The Philippine Islands are small and mountainous. They are close enough to the equator to have hot jungles. Many of the trees in these thick forests can be cut down and sold abroad as fine wood. But the light and hollow bamboo is the most popular building material on the islands.

There are great plantations of sugar, rice, tobacco, coffee, and other crops. But most valuable of all is the plant which gives the thread-like hemp. This hemp is made into rope. Many food crops are grown, and there are numberless kinds of fish and other seafoods to be had, so there is always plenty to eat in the Philippines.

Native homes are built on stilts for protection against floods during the rainy season.

Mountainsides are terraced into small flat fields for growing rice.

Water buffaloes work hard on the farms, and the buffalo cows give milk, too.

Women in the Philippines weave baskets, hats, and fine cloth.

Most of the islands of Japan are small and mountainous. Farms have to be built up on the mountain slopes into tiny, flat fields.

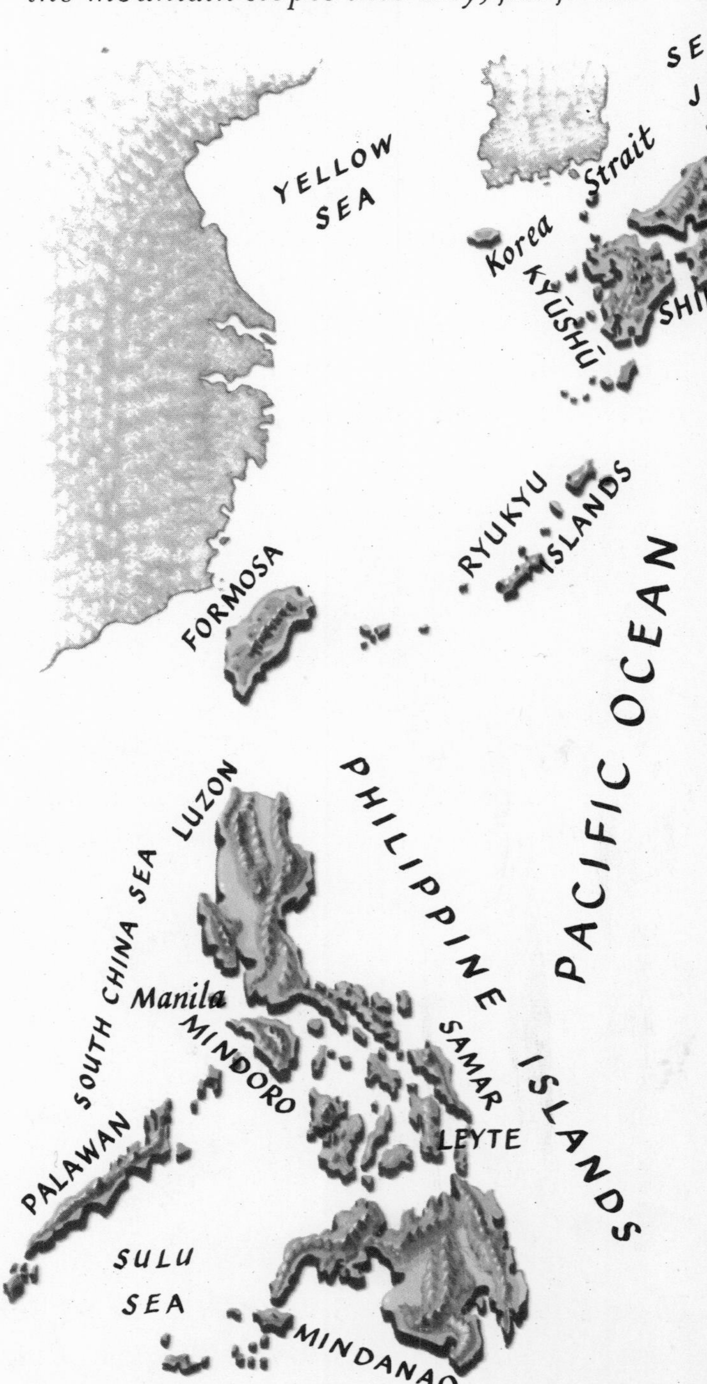

JAPAN

We think of Japan as a part of Asia. Her people belong to the yellow race, like the people of China. And they have many similar ways of doing things.

But the Japanese are cut off from the mainland by water. For many years they also shut themselves away from the rest of the world. They did not want to visit or to be visited by foreigners. They wanted to keep their old ways of doing things.

In modern times, however, they have built factories and schools and have sent some of their young people abroad to other countries to learn modern ways of living.

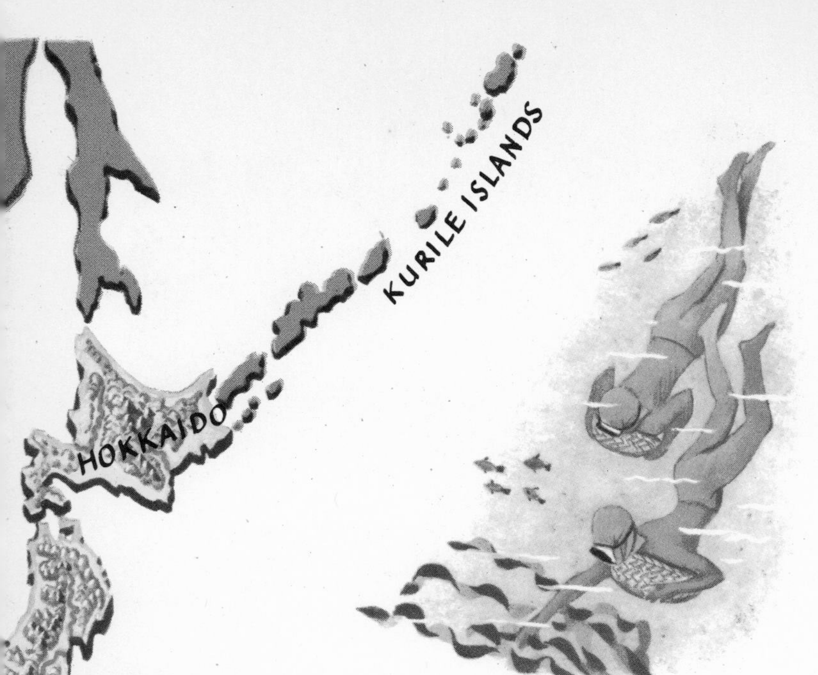

Diving for seaweed is a trade in Japan.

The islands of Japan and the thousands of islands that make up the Philippines lie in the western Pacific Ocean. Here ranges of mountains were covered by seas during the long-ago ages of the world. Now only the mountain peaks show above the surface of the water—as islands.

Women do much of the hard farm work in Japan. Here they are working in the flooded rice fields.

These village people are shown wearing the old-fashioned native costumes of Japan. Nowadays, especially in cities, many people wear Western clothes.

Because the Japanese live on islands, many of them are fishermen. They go far from shore in their little boats.

Here is a Japanese house with sliding paper walls.

Japanese gardens are small but beautiful.

THE EAST INDIES

The East Indies once connected Australia to the continent of Asia. Now most of the land has dropped below the ocean, and only the mountain tops are left.

These islands are rich in woods, oil, gold, silver, and other metals, and in many things that grow.

The weather is hot, but there are welcome breezes, and both plants and animals seem to grow their best on these tropical islands.

Javanese dancers must go to school for long, strict training.

Native houses on Sumatra are built high off the ground.

The great plantations of the East Indies were long owned by Europeans.

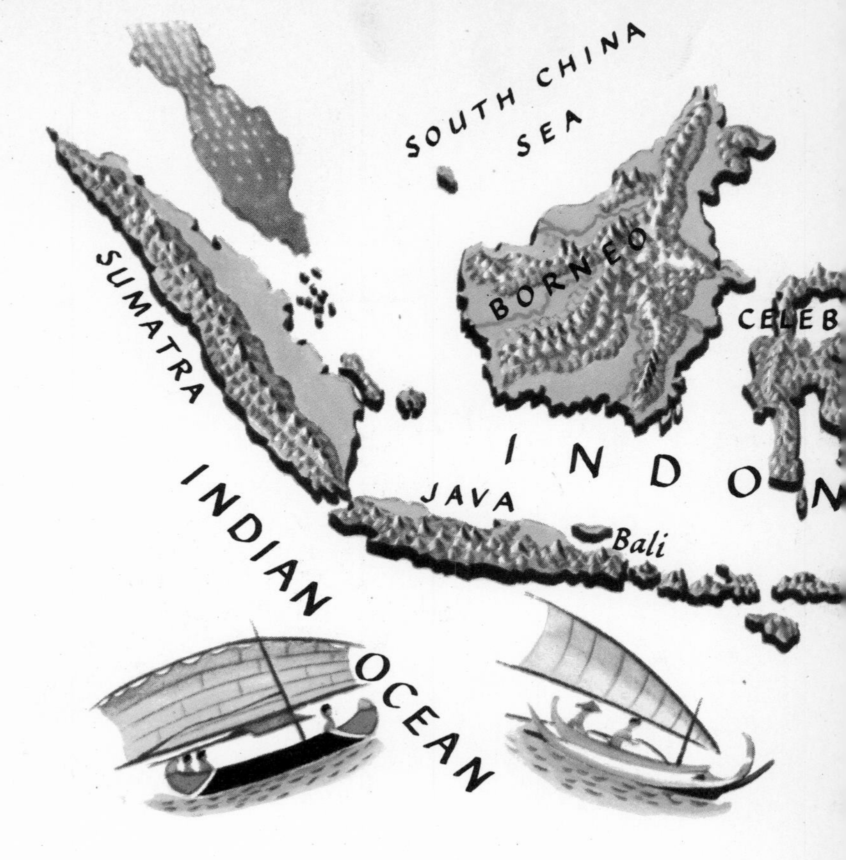

South of the Philippines, off the coast of Asia but farther south, lie the rich islands of the East Indies.

Music comes from strange instruments in the East Indies, and it sounds strange to our ears—strange but beautiful.

Temples on the island of Bali have priestesses as well as priests.

OCEANIA

On the Pacific's tiny scattered islands, known as Oceania, live the world's greatest seamen. These handsome, dark-skinned people have no knowledge of science. They have no big ships. But in their handmade outrigger canoes they can sail for hundreds of miles across the trackless seas straight to a tiny dot of land.

Their homes and clothing are simple, as in all hot lands. Their wants and needs are simple too. The islands give them fruits to eat. The sea gives them fish for the taking. Once or twice a year trading ships bring supplies from the outside world.

PHILIPPINE SEA
SIA
NEW GUINEA
ARAFURA SEA
CORAL SEA

Far out across the Pacific Ocean stretch the tiny dots of land known as Oceania, with hundreds of miles of ocean between.

In these open canoes Polynesian explorers sailed the ocean, settling the scattered islands.

An atoll is a coral island, or a group of them, ringing a quiet lagoon.

Pearl divers lead dangerous lives.

Papeete is the principal city of Tahiti in the Society Islands.

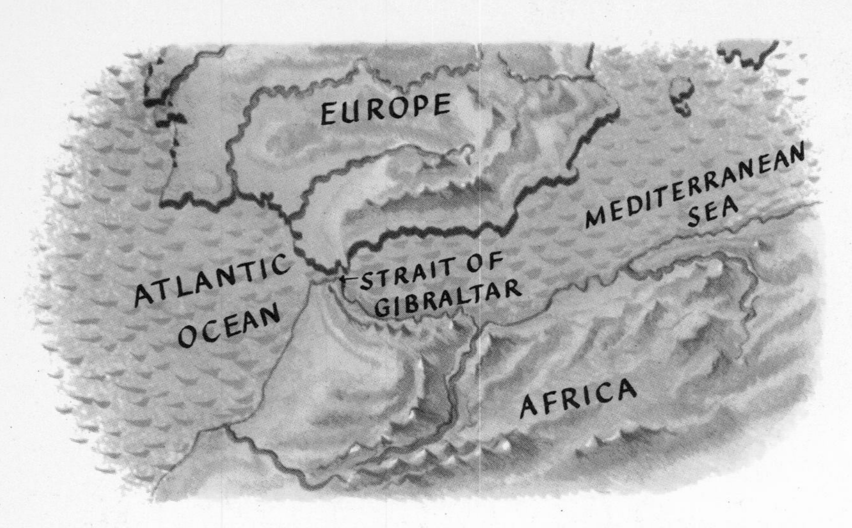

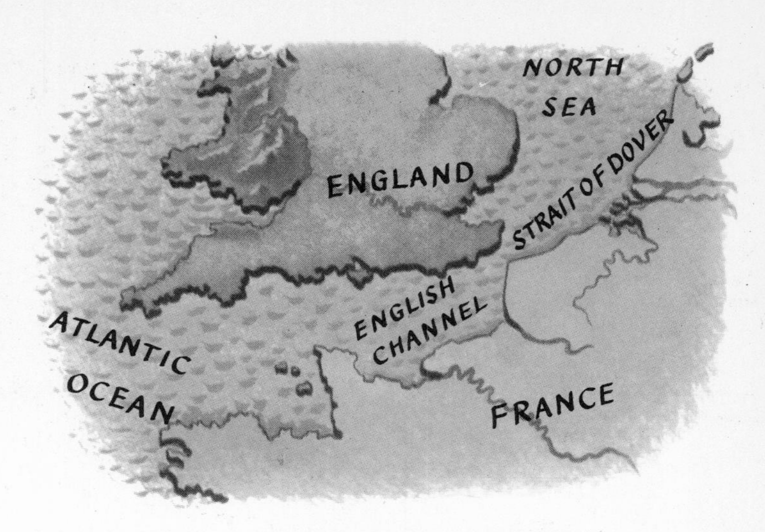

SMALLER BODIES OF LAND AND WATER

Any shape we find in land we will also find in water. Can you see a place in a picture below where two bodies of land are joined by a narrow land strip with water on both sides? A strip of land like this has the strange name of isthmus.

This isthmus joins two continents. Do you see it? It connects North and South America. The narrowest part is called the Isthmus of Panama.

A narrow strip of water with land on both sides, joining two larger bodies of water, is called a strait or channel. One strait separates two continents. Do you see the one on page 23? The Strait of Gibraltar separates Europe from Africa. It connects the Atlantic Ocean with the Mediterranean Sea. The English Channel, between England and France, connects the Atlantic Ocean and North Sea.

Sometimes a piece of land is almost completely surrounded by water, but it is connected to the mainland on one side. This is a peninsula. Let us look at Europe. It is really all a huge peninsula. The rough, rocky knob of Greece is a peninsula with rocky islands all around. So is boot-shaped Italy. It seems to be sliding down from Europe into the sea. And Norway and Sweden are on another European peninsula far to the north.

A smaller peninsula may be called a cape.

And what is a body of water called if it is partly surrounded by land? It is a gulf or a bay. The Gulf of Mexico is partly surrounded by North America; but on its outer side it flows into the Caribbean Sea.

The Isthmus of Panama is a link between North and South America.

The peninsula of Florida borders on the Gulf of Mexico.

The River Seine runs through the lovely city of Paris.

RIVERS

A river, great or small, always has water flowing down a fairly narrow "bed," or channel, toward some sea. Africa has the Nile, which flows four thousand miles through Africa to the Mediterranean Sea. And it has the Congo, which is fed by countless jungle streams on its way to the Atlantic.

South America has the vast Amazon, which winds through trackless jungles and flows at last into the Atlantic through many wide mouths.

The Congo is a water highway into the jungle.

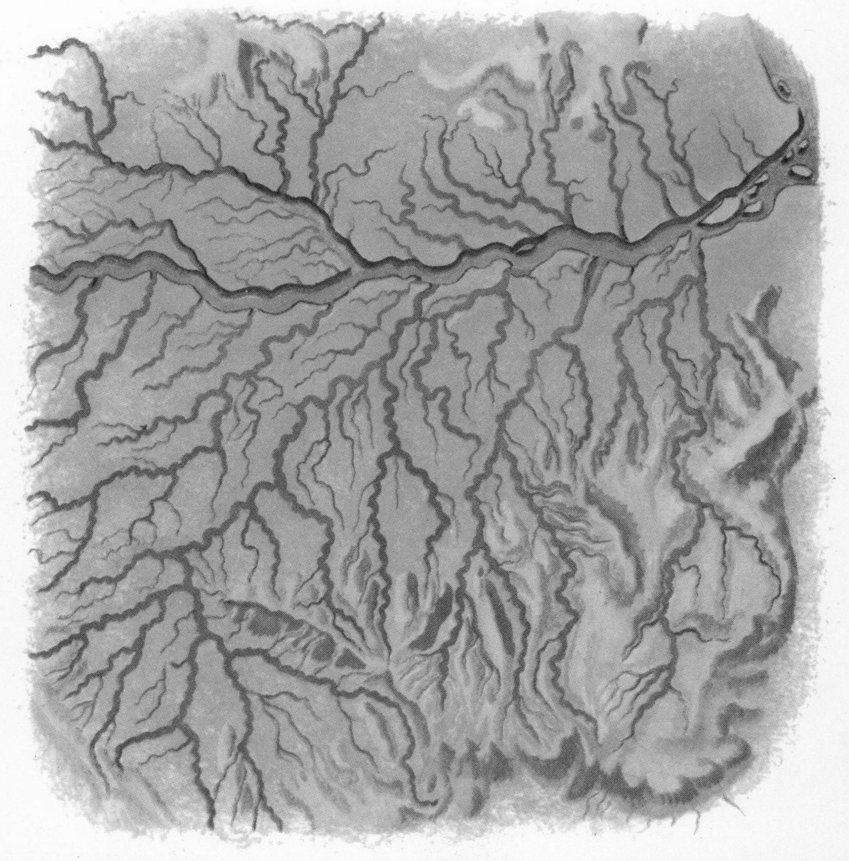

Hundreds of smaller rivers run into the Amazon.

There are shops and houses, whole little cities, on the river boats of crowded China.

North America has the Mississippi, which curves its slow way down to the Gulf of Mexico.

Europe has the busy Rhine and Volga, the Rhone and Danube.

The Mississippi River slides along in great, slow curves. A curve like this is called an oxbow because it looks like an ox-yoke.

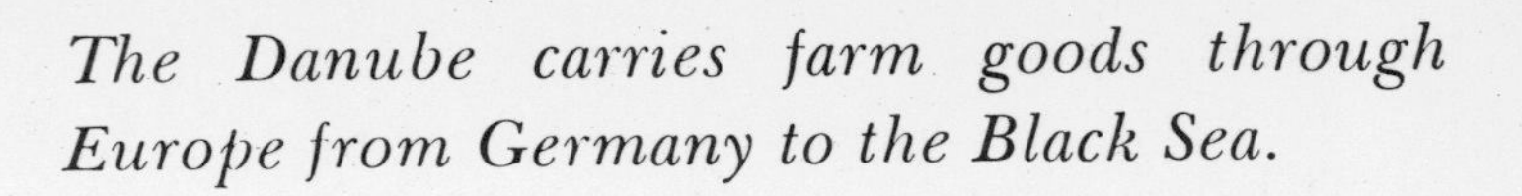

The Danube carries farm goods through Europe from Germany to the Black Sea.

Asia has the Indus, the Ganges, the Yangtze.

And of course every continent has numberless smaller rivers.

People come to bathe in the Ganges River in India as a part of their religion.

Where does a river come from?

Air takes up tiny drops of water from oceans, rivers, and lakes. When water gets into the air in this way, we say it "evaporates." The tiny drops are carried up into the air. They gather into clouds, move over the land, and fall to earth again in drops of rain.

Some rain sinks into the earth. The rest runs along the surface of the earth, always downhill, cutting tiny ditches as it runs. That is one way a river starts.

The water which sank into the earth runs along in underground streams until some pressure forces it up to the surface as a spring. This spring water runs off then in a stream, too.

As many of these tiny streams run downhill, they join together. And they grow into a lively brook.

Now they push more strongly against the earth. And they cut a deeper bed.

A young river runs swiftly and strongly. It can cut down through hard rock as it goes. Through the ages some rivers have cut down through hundreds of feet of rock. The steeper the land it runs through, the faster the river will go.

Every river runs toward a sea or ocean. On the way it may join a larger river. Or other smaller rivers may join it.

As it goes, a river picks up bits of rock and soil. When it comes to the flatter land, near the coast, the river slows down. And as it flows out into the ocean waters, it may leave piles of soil in its path. Land built up in this way is called a delta.

Then there is the water, back in the ocean again. It is ready to be picked up by the air. And to fall as rain. And to start life in a river all over again.

You can read here the story of a river.

MOUNTAINS

The story of a mountain has as much change in it as a river. But it is slower.

The story may start at the bottom of an ocean. There year after year, age after age, bits of shells and sand and soil form a layer, thicker and thicker, on the ocean floor. They are pressed down until they become hard rock.

Rock layer growing.

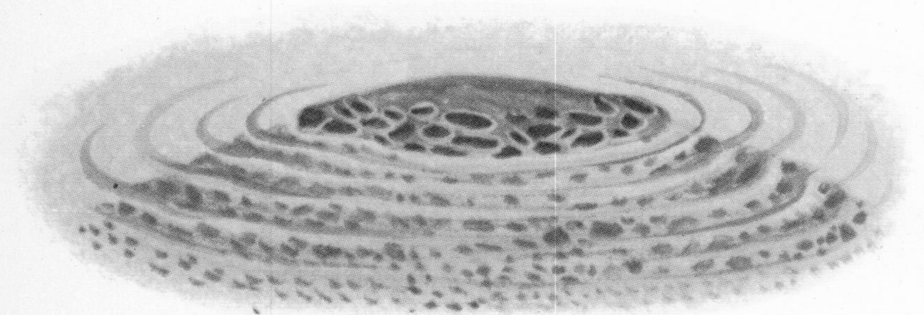

Then some harder rocks press in on this layer from the sides. For ages and ages they squeeze that layer. And little by little it is pushed up, up, out of the water. And it folds and crumples like a sheet of paper you push together between your hands. But these folds of rock are so very big and tall that as they rise up, through the ages, they become mountains.

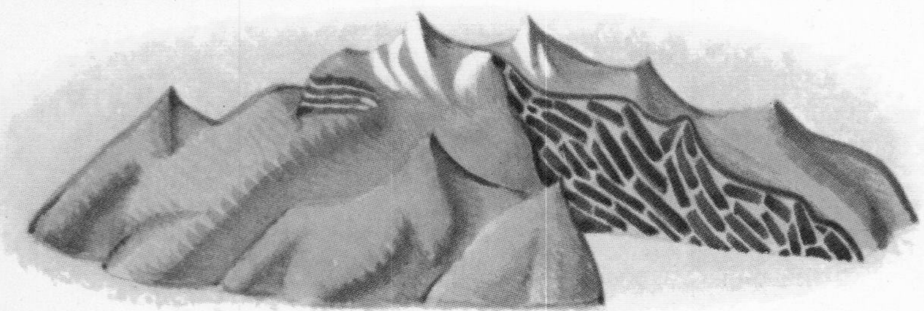

Rocks folded into mountains.

Young mountains always have sharp peaks. But then the wind and water go to work. The wind picks up bits of sand and scrubs at the mountain peaks as you scrub away dirt with cleaning powder. It rubs down the sharp edges.

Wind at work.

Water trickles down the mountain sides. And it wears down paths as it runs. It slips down into cracks and freezes there. And since ice takes more room than water, it forces the rocks farther apart and breaks off some pieces of stone here and there.

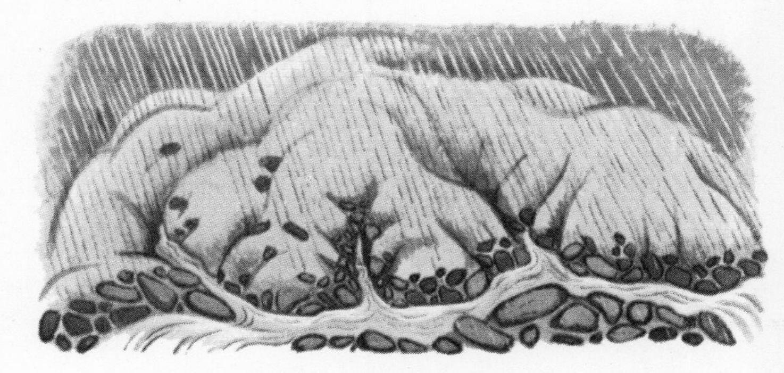

Water at work.

Ages pass. More and more of the sharp peaks have been broken off or worn away. The rock and stone and dirt pile up at the foot of the mountains in smoother slopes.

Plants begin to grow wherever a little soft dirt gathers. As more ages pass, the mountains get rounded on top, with forests growing on their sides.

Still the wind and water keep at work. Through more ages they may wear the mountains down to a rolling plain, quite flat and smooth. It may not even be very high above the sea any more.

But somewhere else in the world, young, sharp-peaked mountains have been pushing up, up, as ages pass.

Volcano erupting.

dead volcano crater

red-hot melted rock

Sometimes, too, the hot gases and melted rocks from deep inside the earth push up through cracks in the earth's surface. The melted rock, called lava, piles up to form new mountains called volcanoes.

Every continent but Australia has at least one great mountain range which pushes high above the rest of the land. Highest of all are the Himalayas of Asia, with Mount Everest, the world's tallest peak. The sharp peaks of these mountains are always white with snow.

The longest range is the great chain which stretches the length of South America as the Andes Mountains, and the length of North America as the Rocky Mountains.

One of the most famous ranges is the Alps of Europe. People from all over the world visit these mountains for their beauty.

And there are many other mountains.

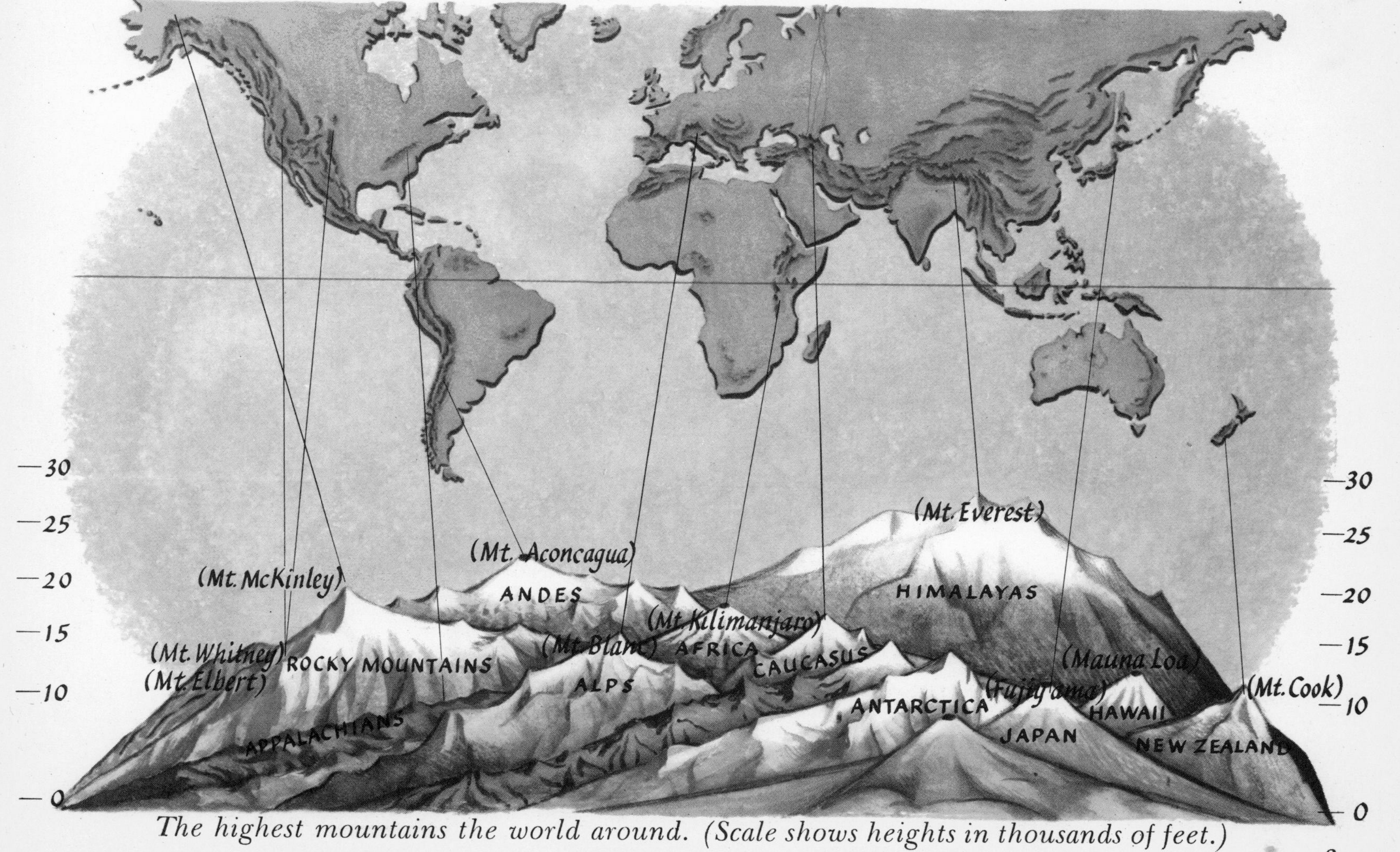

The highest mountains the world around. (Scale shows heights in thousands of feet.)

HIGHLANDS AND LOWLANDS

There are many lower, rounded rolling hills, too.

There are strange flat-topped, steep-sided hills left standing high above the worn-down land around. These are called buttes and mesas.

There are high, flat tablelands and wide stretches of flat land, high or low.

Where there is enough rain and sunshine for grasses and farm crops to grow well, flat land is called "prairie." If it is very dry, it is called "desert." If it is too

cold for trees and most plants, it is called "tundra." It may be a high windy "steppe." Or a low "jungle," damp and hot, where trees, vines, and brush grow in a thick mat.

All these are different kinds of flat lands. The differences are caused by different climates. Now let us see what climate is, and what it means to us.

WHAT MAKES UP OUR CLIMATE

1. Nearness to Poles . . . *or to the Equator.*

2. Lots of rain . . . *or almost none.*

3. Winds that blow . . . *and storms they cause.*

4. Height of land above the seas.

CLIMATE

The kinds of homes and clothes and food people have depend on the climate of the place where they live. Climate is the general kind of weather any place has year after year.

What decides the climate any place will have? All these things:

1. Nearness to the North or South Pole or to the Equator. (The Equator is the imaginary line running around the earth midway between the poles.)
2. How much rain or snow falls.
3. What winds usually blow.
4. How high or low the land is, compared to the level of the seas.
5. What bodies of water are near by.

Now let us see what each of these things has to do with the way people live.

5. Nearness to bodies of water.

The Antarctic is a land of wind and snow and ice. There are no trees, no plants, no people, and only a few animals live there.

Salmon is dried in the short Arctic summer, for winter use.

In winter the husky teams pull heavy sleds long distances over ice and snow.

Greenland's Eskimos raise vegetables in gardens during a short warm season.

LIFE NEAR THE POLES

Around the South Pole is a frozen land called Antarctica. No one at all lives there, though some people have visited it.

A few animals live in the Antarctic—penguins, for example. Seals swim in the cold waters near by.

Great winds blow all the time. There are high snow-covered mountains. But no one ever sees their rocky peaks. For the ice and snow seldom, if ever, melt in the cold Antarctic.

The Arctic is the space around the North Pole. Close to the pole there are only frozen seas. A little farther away there is bare, treeless land where few plants grow, because of the cold and snow.

Eskimos try to gather most of their year's food supply during the short summer. They hunt and fish for most of their food.

The polar bear gives meat and fur.

In summer the Eskimo lives in his sod hut.

The walrus hunt is an exciting adventure.

Some Eskimos live far north, in Alaska and Canada and Greenland, on this barren land. They have few kinds of food. They cannot grow fruits or many vegetables. Their work is hunting polar bears, musk oxen, seals, walrus, and fish. Meat is their principal food.

For light and heat they burn oil they get from animal flesh. Fur makes most of their clothing. The skins of animals cover their tiny boats.

In the winter some build homes of blocks of snow; in the summer, of earth. They travel on snowshoes or on flat dog sleds.

It is the icy climate near the North Pole which gives the people there homes, food, clothing, and means of travel so different from ours.

Hunting the ferocious musk ox has its dangers.

Off go the seal hunters in their kayaks.

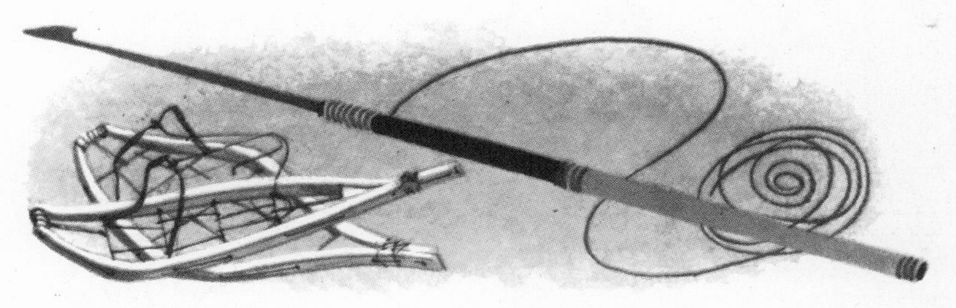

Arctic hunters go on snowshoes and use harpoons.

In winter the Eskimo must travel far for food. He lives then in snow huts called igloos.

Laplanders tend herds of reindeer.

In the hot Amazon valley few clothes are worn by the Indians.

During many months, it rains almost every day in the jungle, so trees and vines grow very fast.

In the deep forests of New Guinea live the birds of paradise

LIFE NEAR THE EQUATOR

Down near the equator the sun always shines its warmest. The long imaginary line of the equator runs across Africa, South America, and Indonesia. It crosses the hot damp jungles of the Amazon River valley and the curving Congo River and dozens of ocean-ringed islands.

In all these places, people live somewhat the same sort of lives, because their climates are similar.

Their homes are small and made of clay or grasses or light wood, because people do not need protection from cold, but only from rain and sun. They have almost no furniture, because they stay inside so little.

Their clothes are few, because they

East Africans haul water in calabashes and make bread from the cassava root.

In Borneo many villages are built in the water on stilts.

do not need to be kept warm. Their skins are dark. Dark skins keep out some of the sun's burning rays.

These people do not need to work very hard to grow food. Crops grow all year round in their gardens. For the land is rich and there is plenty of sunshine and rain. Coconuts and bananas grow on trees without any care at all.

People do not need to work hard for clothes or houses, or for many of the things we need money for in our land. Also, when it is so hot all the time, no one has the energy to work very hard. So we do not find many great factories. There is no need for people to live together in cities. They stay spread out in little villages instead. And they live much more simply than we do.

Market day is a lively day in a village on Bali.

Fish are abundant for food in the Pacific Islands.

Palm trees provide leaves for roofs, and fruits to eat; they give threads for weaving hats and baskets, and sometimes something to sell.

LIVING WITHOUT RAIN

To the right are some homes on Africa's great Sahara Desert. They are wide, low tents. Most desert people live in tents or huts of cloth instead of solid houses. This is because the cloth tents are light and easy to move. And desert people must move around so much.

As you see, there are no trees on the open desert. There is only a little grass.

Arabs live in tents on the Sahara Desert in Africa.

The tent Arabs on march to new pastures.

No farm crops will grow without water. So the desert people—on the Sahara, in Arabia, and in Asia's great Gobi Desert—live by raising sheep and goats. The animals quickly eat up all the grass which springs up after short showers. So every few days or weeks the families must roll up their cloth tents, pile their belongings onto their camels' backs, and move on to a new spot with fresh grass.

Mongols live in felt houses on the Gobi Desert.

Flowers bloom in the desert in western North America.

This is an oasis town in the African desert.

Now and then the tent people come to an oasis. An oasis is a spot on the desert where underground water comes to the surface. The tent people are glad when they see the tall date palms of an oasis. For there they will probably find a town.

There will be cool houses of mud bricks (for there is no wood or stone in the desert to use in building). There will be gardens and orchards of fruit trees. And there will be a market with small shops where they can buy grain and fruits, salt, perhaps a new cooking pot. They will sell their wool and some meat. Best of all, they will fill their leather bags with water. Then off into the desert they will go again, driving their flocks.

The tent people fill their goat skins with water at the well.

The Arabian Desert yields oil for modern industry.

Shepherds watch their flocks on the Mexican desert. Most desert people are wandering shepherds, because not enough food grows in any one place to feed them or their flocks for long.

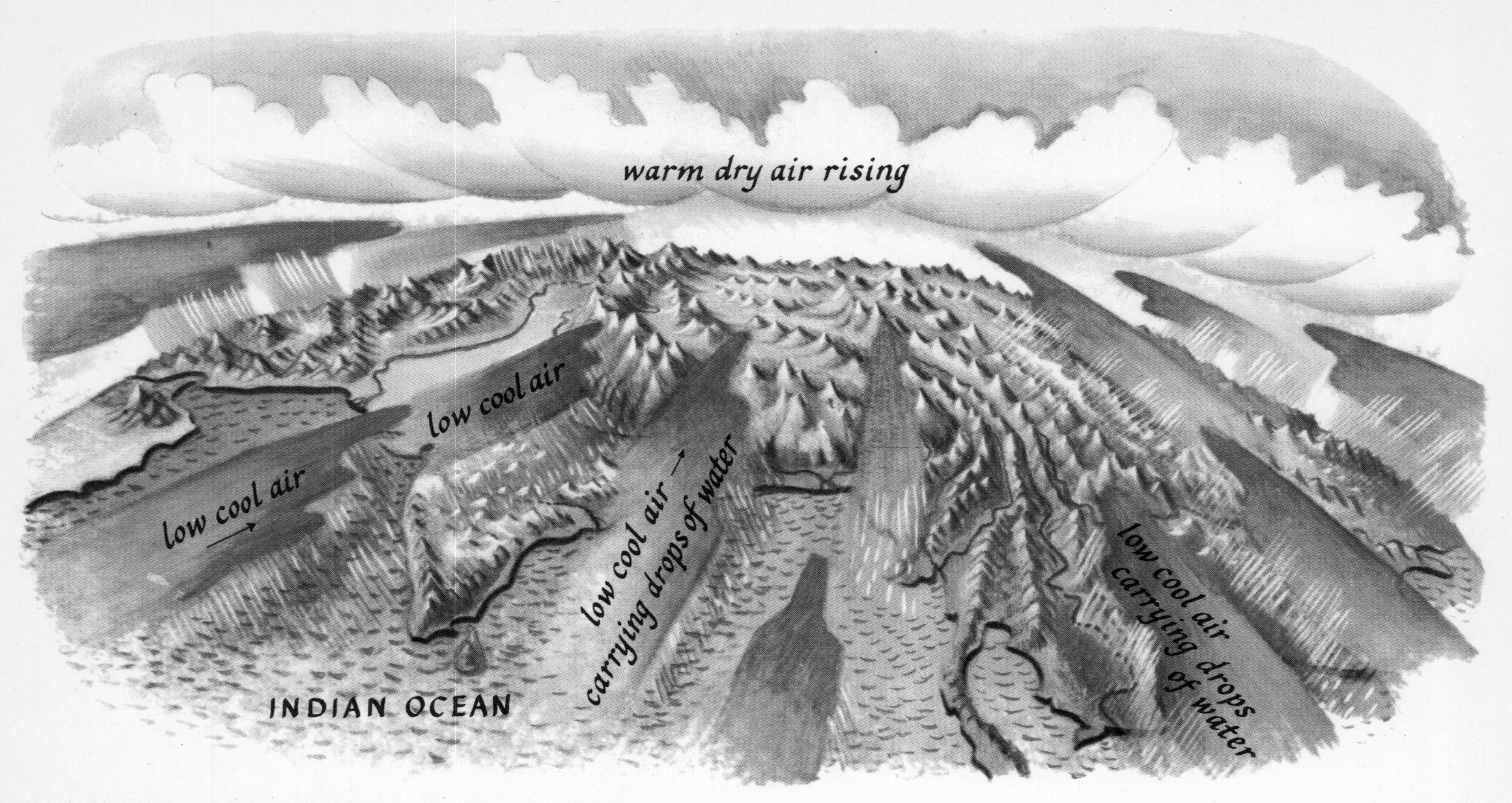

In India and Pakistan the winds control the weather.

The monsoon brings torrential rains.

WINDS THAT BLOW

In India and Pakistan the monsoon is the most important feature of the climate. The monsoon is a warm wind that blows in from the ocean, bringing rain, at certain times of the year. Farmers plan their crops, and people in towns plan the school year and many other things, according to the monsoons. Let us see how this happens.

First of all, what is a wind? It is simply moving air. The air around the earth is always moving. Air sinks down as it grows cooler. As it grows warmer it expands, grows lighter and rises. Then the low cool air rushes in to take its place. And so a wind starts.

Look at India and Pakistan. Up to the north there is a great stretch of land. To the south is an ocean.

In the winter the land is colder than

Rivers in Mexico run almost dry during the dry season.

the ocean. Then the warm air over the ocean rises. And cold, dry air from the northern land sweeps down low over India to take its place. There is such a long dry season that people wish and wait for the summer monsoons that bring the rain.

In the summer the land is warmer than the ocean. So the warm air over the land rises. And the cooler air from the ocean sweeps in low over the land, carrying many drops of water which come down as rain. Then the farmers in the tiny villages work hard to grow good crops with their few tools. For there are so many people in India that no matter how hard they work, there is seldom enough food for all.

Mexico, too, has dry winds from the north (the United States) in the winter, and wet rain-winds from the southern Pacific in the summer.

Spring and summer rains fill the river beds to flooding.

A tornado

Hurricanes turn count

There are other important kinds of winds.

On both sides of the equator, north and south, there are gentle trade winds. They used to blow along the great sailing ships which crossed the seas to trade. And so they got their name.

Then there are the stormy winds which blow toward the Americas over the North and South Atlantic. They

A hurricane

Hurricanes turn clockw

A blizzard

cause dreadful storms around the tip of South America. And sometimes they sweep across Canada and the western United States, bringing torrents of rain or blizzards.

Lesser winds are always at work, bringing cooler or warmer air, and rain and snow in their seasons. We owe most of the day-to-day changes in our weather to winds.

A dust storm

RIVERS IN THE SEA

Look at the little island of Iceland. It is way, way up north in the Atlantic Ocean. It looks as if it would be freezing cold all year long, doesn't it? Most of it is, too. Most of the high center of the island is covered with huge fields of ice and snow which never melt. No one lives there.

But Iceland's harbors never freeze over. And the people in its neat, pleasant though treeless towns near the shore enjoy fairly mild winters. This is because a stream of warm water from the sunny Gulf of Mexico far away flows up across the Atlantic and along the shores of Iceland. It is called the Gulf Stream.

The great winds of the world push the waters of the oceans before them. These streams of water pushed along by the winds are called currents. They change the climates of the lands they touch. The Gulf Stream is one of these currents.

The warm Gulf Stream keeps Iceland's harbors open though they are far up North.

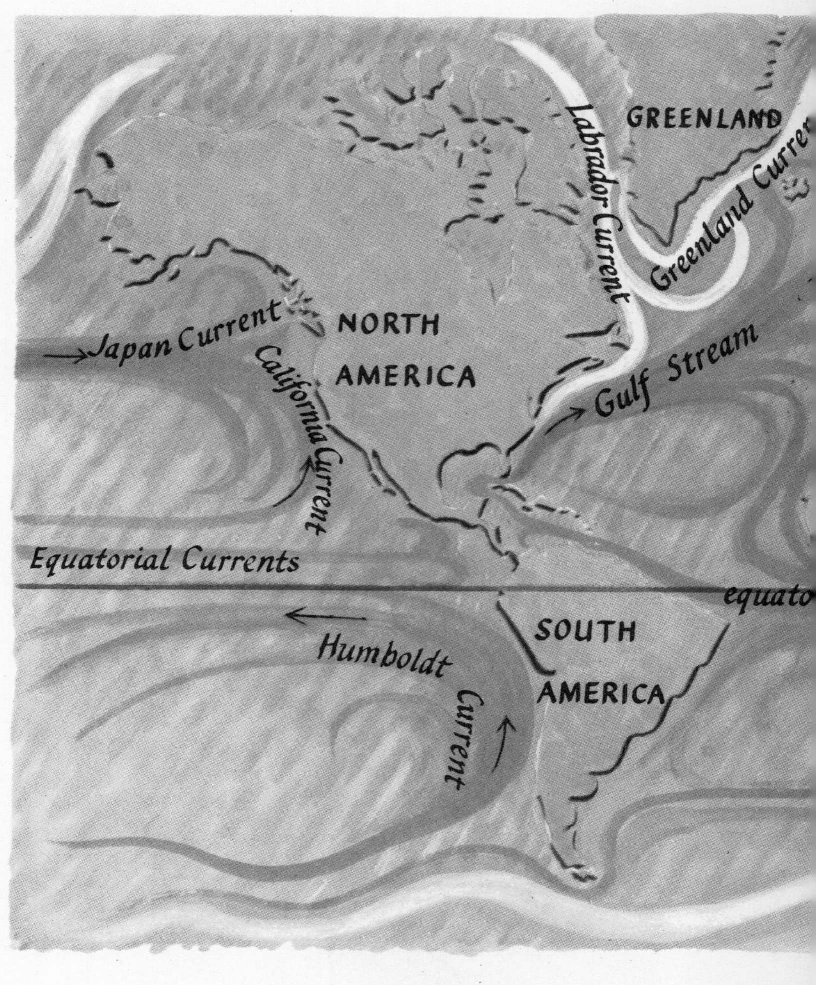

From a plane flying above, you can see the "river" of the Gulf Stream flowing through the Atlantic Ocean.

The warm waters of the Japanese current keep the Japanese Islands from becoming very cold.

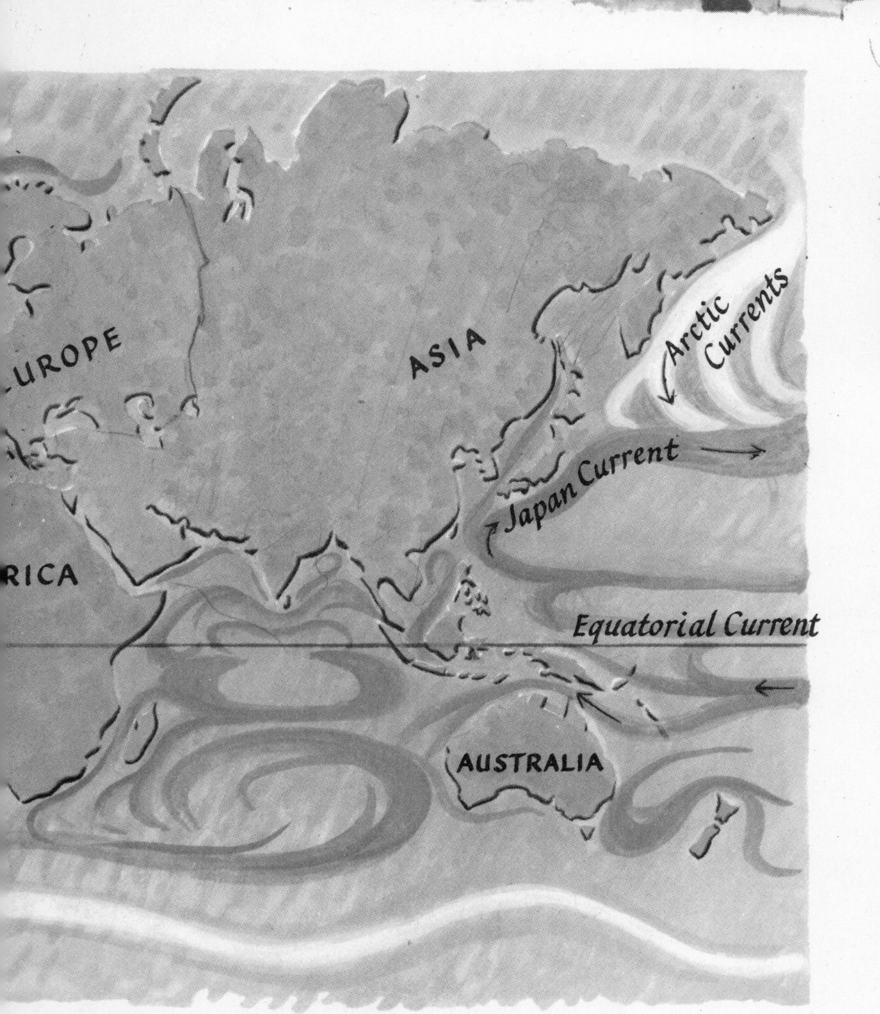

This warm current makes it possible for fishermen to fish all year round near Iceland, and for farmers to raise crops near its shores. The Gulf Stream also warms the climate of Great Britain, Norway, and western Europe.

On the other side of the world, the islands of Japan stretch far north in the Pacific Ocean. But a warm current from the equator sweeps northward along their shores. And the warm waters keep the islands from becoming very cold.

There are cold currents, too. Look at the long west coast of South America. Much of the southern coast is cool and bare. And why? A cold current from the icy waters of the Antarctic Ocean sweeps up along those shores.

So "rivers in the sea" change climates in all parts of the world.

An icy Antarctic current makes South America's western coast chilly and bare.

Villages nestle in the valleys of the Swiss Alps.

Mountain men in Afghanistan use yaks to carry heavy loads up steep, rocky trails.

UP IN THE MOUNTAINS

Here is a village high in the mountains. It is a village in the Alps. But there are many mountain villages that look something like this, in many different countries. This is because they are all built to suit their climate, high in the mountains.

The air is thinner and colder in the mountains than it is down close to the sea. In the winters there is a good deal of snow. Houses must be sturdily built, with steep roofs, so the snow will slide

Summer pasture is high in the mountains.

off and not form a heavy layer which might crush the house. Most mountain houses are made of wood, because on the lower slopes of many mountains there are heavy forests.

Fields are small and steep. There are no big farms. Most people keep cows and goats, because these flocks can feed from rough pastures. In the winter they feed on stored-up hay. But in the spring and summer, as the snow melts on the mountainsides, they go up to eat the fresh grass of higher pastures.

Japanese farmers build up mountain slopes into small, flat terrace fields.

Mountain climbers like to climb difficult peaks. They are roped together so that if one starts to fall, the others can hold him up.

Some Norwegian mountain men work in the forests, cutting trees for lumber in the winters.

Swiss mountain folk do fine wood carving during the long winters.

It is harder to build roads and railroads in the mountains than on level ground. So many mountain people seldom get far from home.

Everyone travels on skis in the snowy Swiss winters.

Winters are long and snowy in the mountains. The people of the Swiss Alps keep busy working with their hands, at woodcarving, embroidery, and other fine work.

In Norway the men go fishing or cut wood in the forests. And for the women, there is butter and cheese to make.

Most mountain people learn to travel over the snow on skis. They can slide ever so swiftly down the slopes. Everything in their lives is planned to suit the climate of their homes.

Stockholm, in Sweden, is a busy seaport.

DOWN BY THE SHORE

This city is built beside the sea. All around the world there are cities which are like it in some ways because they are on the seacoast or an ocean shore.

These are the great seaports of the world. Ships steam into their harbors to unload cargoes on the long wharfs. They steam out from the shelter of the harbor into the open sea, loaded with the goods that country has to sell.

There is always a busy section down beside the water in any port. Long piers push out into the water, with docks or spaces for ships between.

Often railroad tracks run down to the piers or wharfs. Then goods can be quickly loaded and unloaded from trains.

Usually big businesses have warehouses close by, to store some of the goods which travel by water.

Often there are factories in port cities, too. There things are made to be shipped away.

Near by is the busy center of the city, with its offices and stores. Then, often up on higher ground, are the homes. Many people have made great fortunes trading by sea. So most port cities have many fine big homes.

This is a typical seaport. See the piers and docks. See the railroad tracks. See the warehouses for storing goods. See the factories. See the business section. See the homes beyond.

There are many small towns and villages on the sea shores and ocean coasts, too. There most of the families get their living from the sea. Many of the men fish. They go out into the rough seas in small boats, cast their nets into the water, and bring back their

The lighthouse warns ships at sea of hidden rocks, day and night.

Fishing boats like all of these go out on some waters every day.

A harbor must have sheltered, quiet waters for ships. Some harbors have islands or curving shorelines to shelter them. Some have man-made sea walls.

catch to sell. Others are boat builders. Or they pack or can the fish to ship away and sell. Some have shops to sell fishing and ship supplies. One way or another, most of the families in towns along the shore depend for their living on the sea.

Working in a fish cannery is one way to make a living near the sea.

Big ships are built by modern factory methods, but many fine smaller craft come from small boatyards.

There are many fishing villages on the Atlantic coasts. This one is in France.

Many seashore spots are summer resorts, where people from far away come to play and rest and swim. For an ocean or sea keeps the weather milder along the shore. The winters are not as cold as they are inland, though winds and storms may be fierce. And the summers are not as hot as in other places. So people from the hot cities inland like to go to the shore, where night breezes are cool.

Ocean beaches are pleasant places to go on hot summer days.

A New Jersey river; U. S. A.

LIFE ALONG THE RIVERS

A boat whistle hoots. Warning bells clang. Up goes a big bridge. And down the river chugs a steamboat trailing a long row of loaded flat barges. These barges are the freight trains of our great rivers. They carry coal, food, cattle, all sorts of goods, along the river highways of the world.

Many cities are built along great rivers. Often the banks are walled with stone or brick or concrete to keep the river from washing away bits of the city or flooding it.

Often cities have parks along the river, with places for people to sit and rest. But the river banks are busy, too. There are docks where boats load and unload. And often factories are built close to the river.

Some factories use river water in their work; others use the power of the river water to turn wheels to turn machines. Or the water power may be turned into electricity in great plants, and the electricity then is used in factories as well as in homes to do all kinds of work.

The Seine in Paris, France, is beautifully lined with trees.

Basel in Switzerland is one of the busiest river-ports in Europe.

Many of our great cities are built at the mouths of rivers.

Rivers pass through miles and miles of countryside, too, between the cities and towns.

Where a river runs through a great forest, it may be used in lumbering. Logs are dragged to the river and floated downstream in great loads to the sawmill.

Where small rivers or streams run through woodland or quiet country, fishermen like to camp near the banks to try their luck. They may fish from small boats or from the shore. Or they may wade out into the stream.

There are some rivers along which fishing is done as a big business. In big canneries the fish are prepared for sale. These canneries provide jobs for whole villages of people.

Where rivers run through farmland they are important, too. Often the melting snow in the high land where the

This old-time mill grinds wheat into flour. It uses river water to turn its mill wheel.

Levees are extra walls built up to hold the river in its place when it is running high at flood time.

This factory makes fine leather from animal skins. It uses river water to wash the skins many times.

river starts fills it to overflowing with water. Then, rushing down through the countryside, the river may overflow its banks and cause a flood.

In some places floods cause great losses. Men keep watch night and day along the banks to see how much the water is rising. They build walls of earth, perhaps with nets of steel for strength, to hold the river in its place.

Trees cut in the forest are brought to ponds like this and are slid into the water. Then they are floated down the river to the sawmill.

This big electric power plant uses the power of river water to make electricity.

Rivers provide pleasant picnic spots in the countryside.

A dam holds back extra river water and lets it through as it is needed. Ditches called irrigation canals lead river water through the dry fields, so that it nourishes the plants' roots.

In other places these floods are eagerly awaited. The yearly flooding of the River Nile keeps bringing new richness to the soil of the Nile valley in Egypt, year after year.

Instead of letting the river waters wash over the land just by chance, men may build dams. These dam walls hold back the extra water in great lakes or ponds. Then little by little the water is allowed to run through as it is needed. It flows down the river. It flows out into canals. It is led along through the dry country to farms where little rain falls. The river water runs through the fields in ditches and helps the crops to grow.

These dams and supplies of river water are helping to change the climate of some sections. They are changing deserts into farmlands.

Ancient irrigation methods are still being used to water many fields in Egypt.

LIFE ON THE FARM

In almost every country of the world there are farms. But of course they are not all alike. The climate of each country decides what kind of farms there will be.

What can be grown on a farm depends on the kind of weather, the kind of soil, and the countryside.

You may live on a flat open farm where the soil is rich enough for corn and wheat. Your land may be rich enough for tobacco or sandy enough for potatoes or wet enough for rice. Perhaps the weather is warm enough for cotton or for oranges and lemons.

Maybe you have a small farm where you try to grow most of the things you need to live. You keep a few cattle for milk and meat and you grow some corn to feed them. You have a team of horses and you grow some oats for them. You keep one field in grass for pasture for the animals. And you grow some grass or clover to cut for hay.

You have a big garden to grow vegetables for your family. You have a few fruit trees, some chickens and pigs. You may even keep a few sheep for their wool.

You must have some "cash crop," too. This is a crop you grow to sell, so you will have some money for buying supplies. You may cut trees in your wood lot and sell wood. Perhaps you sell some wheat or corn or barley or oats. Or it may be grapes or other fruit, depending on where your farm is.

This kind of farm, where almost everything the family needs is grown on the place, is not found so much any

A big flat wheat farm u

more in the United States. Usually it is simpler to buy most things in town and to grow just a few things you can grow especially well.

There are many different kinds of farms scattered over the world. Some are very small. Many countries have so many people that they are very crowded. A farmer can have only a very small farm. He may have just one small field. Sometimes he does not live on his farm. He lives in a near-by village and goes out to his field each day to work.

Some farms have strange shapes. The

Tobacco needs special care. It is started in covered hot beds, before being set out. Later the ripe leaves are hung up to "cure" in slat-sided sheds.

Farms along the St. Lawrence River, with narrow fields sloping to the water's edge.

rge combines for harvesting.

fields may be divided into long narrow strips. And each farmer has a strip. Or in the mountains the slopes may be built up into little flat fields shaped like fans. These are called terraces.

Farmers may own their own land. They may work for themselves. They may all work together on a farm that belongs to the nation. Or they may work for a man who owns a great deal of land.

We find these huge farms owned by one man, with a lot of farmers working for him, most often where just one crop is raised to sell.

Many famous wines come from grapes grown in the vineyards of France.

A family farm may grow most of the things the family needs.

Rice needs very wet soil. Rice fields are flooded when the young plants start to grow.

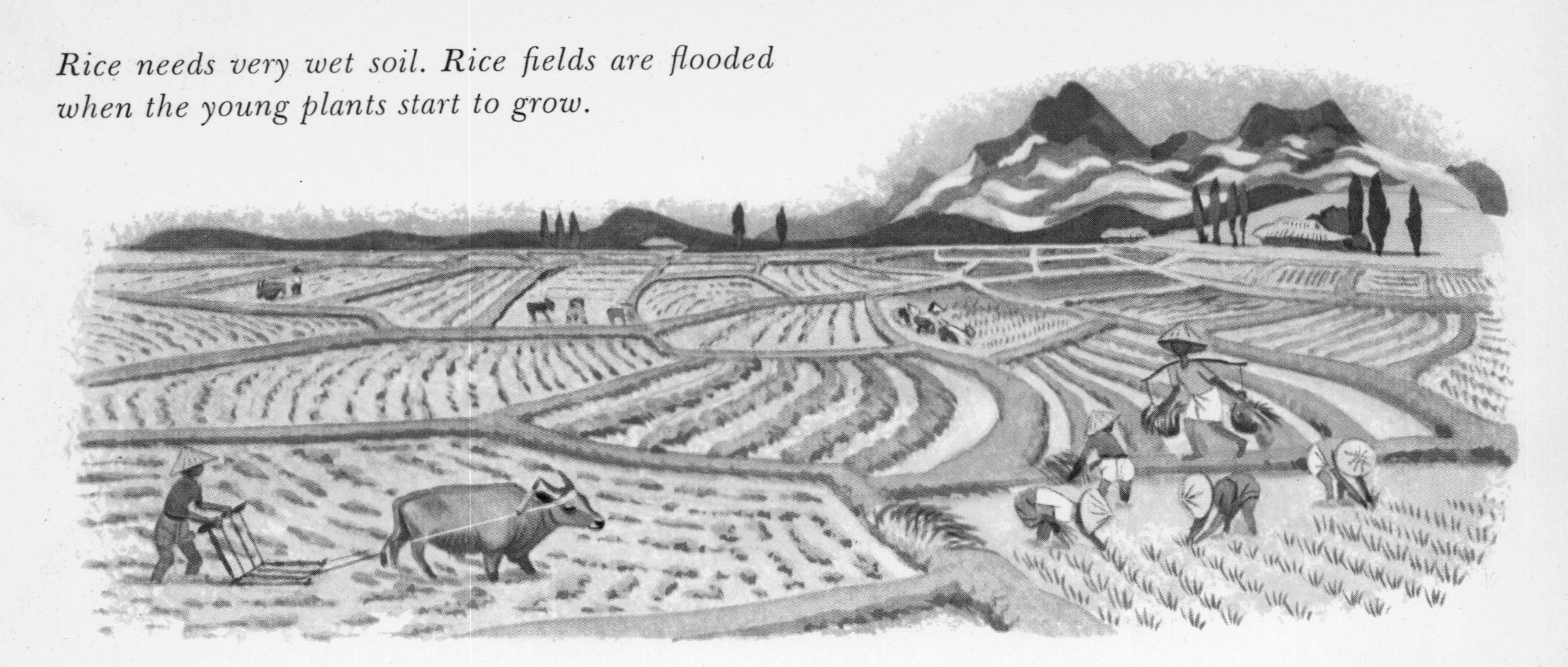

Cotton crops are often "dusted" with poison to kill harmful bugs, especially boll weevils.

It may be sugar or pineapples on a plantation in Hawaii, tea or rice in China and the Philippines, cotton in Egypt or the United States. Raising cattle may be the work on a cattle ranch in the western United States. Or raising sheep on a sheep station in Australia. These are kinds of farms, too.

Whatever your crops or weather or kind of countryside, life on a farm is different from life in a city.

On a farm you are not crowded in

A big ranch, which is a farm that raises cattle, has few fields or fences. Its land is mostly open range.

Sugar cane is here being cut on a plantation in the Hawaiian Islands.

with thousands of other people. You see fewer people. You see more open spaces. There is a lot of hard work to be done. But there is usually not as much of a hurry about it as in a city.

You watch the seasons as they change. You make friends with the animals. You learn to know trees and plants.

A farm does not have the bright lights and noise and excitement of a city. But millions of people find it is a good life, life on a farm.

Pineapples grow well in the even climate of the beautiful Hawaiian Islands.

Orange and lemon groves need warm weather. Their trees have leaves and blossoms and fruit all year around.

EXPLORING IS FUN

Geography is the study of life on the earth. It is the study of hills and rivers and lakes and trees, of how they change and grow. And it is the study of people and how they live, near the sea, in the great cities, in the mountains, on deserts and on prairie farms. It shows how their work and their homes and food and clothing all depend somewhat on the plants and animals and the kind of countryside around them.

To build their homes, people use whatever the country around them offers—wood or stone or bricks or mud; grass and palm leaves or blocks of snow.

People eat what the near-by land and water provide—fish if they live near lakes, rivers or sea; game if they live in a wide-open land where wild animals still roam; fruits which happen to grow near by; and whatever grains or animals they find their countryside raises best.

Clothing, too, differs from land to land. People wear furs where the land is

very cold and they cannot grow plants from which to make cloth. They wear wool if there are shepherds raising sheep near by, or if they can trade something for wool; they may wear very little clothing at all if they live in a very hot land.

They may travel by sled or horseback, by camel or airplane or river boat. It all depends on where they live.

There are very few people who, like us, can trade with all the world. We can eat fruits and spices and drink coffee and tea from many lands. We can wear wool and silk and felt and straw which have come to us from people far away. And we can travel wherever we wish, to visit friends in all parts of the world, by ship or train or plane, or in the pages of a book.

Traveling to find out how other people live and to make friends with them is called exploring. And exploring is a kind of fun we can enjoy all our lives long.

INDEX